Irish History for the Inquisitive

Stories of intrigue, hope, farce and devastating loss.

Clive Scoular

Published in 2015 by
Clive Scoular,
Killyleagh, County Down

ISBN 978-0-9574626-5-6

The author gratefully acknowledges the unstinting help in the
presentation, design and layout of this book given by his partner,
Thomas Johnston.

for Eilish Johnston

a loving mother and mother-in-law

Irish History for the Inquisitive

An Introduction and an Explanation

FOR YEARS I have been reading all sorts of stories about Ireland's history and the people who made Ireland what it is. I have shared these tales with countless groups of people, young and not so young, and I have enthralled them with the excitement, the unbelievableness and the pure thrill of so many events which you could hardly believe to be true, examples of which are contained in these following episodes from our vivid, vibrant and varied history.

To me these stories are for an inquisitive people like the Irish. To me this word epitomises the Irish – a nation of bright and clear headed people - and one which encourages people to want to hear something a bit different and asking the question – well did this really happen in Ireland? – or perhaps something like – well this could only happen in Ireland.

I have written short pieces about a number of interesting and intriguing events which have occurred throughout our past, recent and not so recent. These are stories I love and which never fail to astonish and captivate me. We all know a bit about the famine and its aftermath; the blitz, which killed so many Belfast folk during World War Two, and maybe something about the Black and Tans. But what about the theft of the Irish Crown Jewels; the thrills involved in the Fremantle Mission when prisoners were sprung from prison in Australia and brought to America and the unbelievable tales of feckless German spies in Ireland?

Does anyone know anything about the Great Flu, which killed countless millions of people immediately after World War One, or about the gun running to Unionists and Nationalists in Ireland prior to that conflict? And can you believe that an entire village was stolen from the south coast of Ireland in the early 1600s?

I have also included mini biographies of four of Ireland's greatest personalities – our own St Patrick and then the geniuses who were WB Yeats, JM Synge and Sean O'Casey.

I freely admit that my selection of stories is what you might describe as a quirky one. But I defy any of you not to be thrilled and inspired by my choice of historical vignettes. Sit back and read and have your innate inquisitiveness thoroughly satisfied.

Clive Scoular
Killyleagh
September 2015

Patrick

Ireland's courageous, stubborn and steadfast patron saint

Statue of St Patrick on the hill of Saul, county Down

PEOPLE IN IRELAND, and wherever the Irish live and congregate, have some idea and notion of who Patrick was and where he came from. But what are the facts? From the outset we need to appreciate that commonly repeated stories about Patrick are notoriously unreliable. He only left us his Confessio and his Letter and after that much has to be left to different interpretations – in other words lots of people will tell you that theirs is the gospel truth about this great and good Christian man.

He was probably born around the year 385AD somewhere in Roman Britain. We do know that his was a Christian family who were quite well to do. His father's name was Calpurnius and, although he could have been born in Dumbarton, in Scotland, or in Wales, there are those who believe he came from the mainland of Europe from such divergent places as Spain and Boulogne in France. However, my best guess, after reading extensively about him, is that his birthplace was somewhere in the Severn Valley near Gloucester.

He was a healthy youth who, in his own words, was certainly no saint. And, despite his Christian upbringing, he turned away from God in his teenage years. And then his life was turned upside down when he and other members of his family were kidnapped and spirited away to Ireland. This was a regular occurrence in those days. Men who needed workers or slaves simply sailed round the coastlines of the British Isles and captured men, women and children. There seemed little protection from these pirate ships and it was Patrick's bad luck that his family was taken. To add to the boy's distress, he was soon separated from his parents and taken up the east coast of Ireland and put ashore somewhere on the shores of Larne Lough, as it is known today.

He was taken to Slemish Mountain and given the job of minding sheep on that desolate hillside for a man called Miliucc. Nothing much is known of this man although it seems that the young Patrick was simply left alone to get on with his work as a shepherd. Presumably he had food to eat and some sort of shelter in which to sleep. For six long years he endured the vagaries of the weather and suffered the cold, the wind and the snow. But he enjoyed mixing with the local people and learned to speak their language. He also returned to his faith and learned to pray once again. His life, though decidedly tough, was tempered with the knowledge that he had some friends and that he had found his Saviour once again. This call was to help him in later years to convert the Irish although he did not, of course, realise this at the time. Nights and days were long upon the mountainside and the young Patrick, as we would say today, had to bide his time.

Escape from Ireland – a call from God

After these six long years, Patrick, who would have been in his early twenties by then, answered a call from God to get up and leave Slemish and his sheep. In those days it would have been a very courageous move to make. Patrick gathered his few belongings and headed south. He could perhaps have gone back to the shore where he had landed to find a boat that would take him away from Ireland.

But this would have been risky, as the sailors could well have known Miliucc and taken Patrick back into captivity. Instead the strong-willed Patrick headed much further south and walked almost 200 miles to a little port somewhere in modern day county Wicklow.

Here, however, trouble began. No one was prepared to take him on board their ship. He was an unknown and none of the ships' captains wanted to oblige Patrick by taking him with them. Patrick prayed and let those around him see that he was praying. In due course of time he was eventually offered a passage, having in the meantime converted a number of the sailors. Patrick himself was still uncertain about his faith but continually asked God to forgive him his transgressions, which he admitted were many and great. He soon discovered that the boat he was on was bound for modern day France and he was required to look after a number of Irish wolfhounds.

It is really a complete mystery as to where he landed in France. A measured guess would have been somewhere on the west coast and he described the place to be nothing more than desert. He learnt that the Vandals had recently laid bare the entire country and so he had trouble finding a place to stay. But his determination to follow the Lord's call took him to the centre of France, somewhere near Auxerre, where he went on to train for the priesthood. This is a whole part of Patrick's life that seems hard to believe, for where would he have found priests and some sort of seminary in the middle of France after the country's devastation by warring hordes?

Be that as it may, he now was a priest and he headed off for the south coast of France somewhere not far from modern day Nice. And it is when he was there that the story of Patrick expelling the snakes from Ireland might have arisen. This is a possible scenario. Patrick is listening to a priest friend of his who has recently returned from service on one of the Lerins islands off the south coast of France. Whilst there, he was involved in the extermination of vermin from the island that were threatening the lives of its inhabitants. Amongst the pests to be put down were a number of snakes. Patrick asked how the job had gone and was told it had been entirely successful. One can therefore imagine that, throughout Patrick's perambulations across Ireland in his later years, he would have told stories, around an evening campfire, about the places he had visited during his ministry. One can imagine that the yarn about the snakes and their expulsion from Lerins could, like the well-known Chinese whisper 'send reinforcements we're going to advance' becoming 'send three and fourpence we're going to a dance', could easily have become 'we've sent away the snakes from the island off France' to 'we've just expelled the snakes from our island of Ireland'. Well it is a possibility and why could we not believe it?

In truth there is not really much known about Patrick's time in France – it did seem to last a fair time; he certainly became a priest whilst there and he may even have become a bishop during those years, probably in the year 431AD. Then the Lord called him back to Ireland. One can imagine Patrick's reaction – something like 'I'm not too keen on that move for I didn't really enjoy my first time there.' But, being a devoted follower of his Lord, Patrick set off on what were to become the most rewarding and fulfilling years of his life.

We can now consider Patrick's movements after leaving France until his eventual arrival in Ireland. Firstly he had to ensure that his fellow priests in France were ready and prepared to carry on God's work there and secondly he felt the need to encourage those converts he had made to continue to lead a Godly life. Having satisfied himself on these important issues, he set out for Britain and then for Ireland.

What kind of man was Patrick and what did he look like?

Contrary to many opinions it seems likely that Patrick did not have a beard but was clean-shaven with a tonsure. He would have been of medium build and would have worn a variety of clothes. He would, of course, have worn his clerical robes when the occasion required it but, during his long and demanding travels throughout the country, he would have had cloaks and trews depending on the vagaries of the Irish weather. And, as time went on, he would have had lots of minor injuries caused by fights and accidents from falls from chariots for example and would have often looked battered and bruised. He was a determined man; he did not, as we would say today, suffer fools gladly; he spoke his mind; he was an irritable man but, most importantly, he would never have bowed down to anyone except God.

Having thus described this great man, and future beloved saint of Ireland, we know he was someone who liked getting things done and expected his entourage of men and women to do the same. We must now imagine his return to Ireland at the beginning of his mission to Christianise the Irish. It would have been in the year 432AD when he set sail. It has been said that he had expected to land somewhere on the coast of county Wicklow but the wind and weather pushed his boat as far up as the narrows which run between the modern day villages of Portaferry and Strangford and that he was deposited close to Saul inside Strangford Lough. We can perhaps imagine how he felt. It probably did not matter to him that he had landed where he did for all he wanted to do was get on with the work the Lord had set out for him. As he climbed up the hill from his landing site close to the Slaney River, he found that he had arrived in quite a populated area and immediately encountered the local chieftain who was called Dichu. Being the kind of man Patrick was he simply came up to a fairly bemused Dichu, who was hardly expecting a large number of strangers to be visiting, and looked him straight in the eye. Neither man wanted trouble so Patrick asked Dichu if he could offer him with a place to stay until he had figured out his plan for his journeys throughout the country. Dichu obliged and the 'barn' at Saul became Patrick's first home in Ireland and was his first consecrated church. Patrick and Dichu came to like one another which pleased both men as well as the local people and the followers of Patrick. In fact Dichu was soon converted to Christianity and was baptised soon afterwards.

Patrick's remarkable Irish journey

When Patrick and his friends left Saul no one could have guessed the scale of his travels. In the 25 or so years that he spent in Ireland until his death, he covered over 90% of the entire island – the only exception being a few of the counties in the south west. We must not forget that Ireland was, at that time, 80% tree covered with very few tracks on which to travel. He would have had to sail down rivers and coastlines, for there were no bridges to cross them, and either walked or ridden on a cart or an unsprung chariot across extremely difficult terrain. Patrick's followers, who would have included members of his own family, together with cooks, smiths, clerics and bodyguards, as well as women whose job it was to sew and mend their vestments, would constantly have been looking for places to stay and prepare their food which would have been a real and constant challenge.

But Patrick was never put off for he knew what he had been sent to Ireland to do – and that was to convert the Irish. He realised that the local people were decent enough but had not yet had the chance of hearing the word of God. He also had the foresight to bring with him a number of young men he was preparing for Holy Orders and these new priests were to become his right hand men in his mission. We can imagine, for a moment, a week in the life of Patrick and his disciples. They were perhaps travelling through the midlands of the country with its dense woodlands and raging river torrents; food would have been hard to find so they would have had to lay traps to ensnare some of the indigenous wild animals; time would need to have been spent with his young ordinands and then there was the typical Irish weather with which to contend. Yet they moved on with their goal in mind – to convert the locals to the way of Christ.

And in the midst of all this strenuous, yet rewarding, work, Patrick was also able to introduce the Latin alphabet to the Irish, since Ireland at that time had only, and in limited measure, the Druids' Ogham script. He was a truly remarkable man whose legacy lives on.

Enter some warring chieftains

Patrick was soon to find out that all would not be plain sailing for his mission in Ireland. There were chieftains who ruled different parts of the country and, if he was going to cover as much of Ireland as he could, he would surely encounter some of these despots. And he certainly did. On arriving at the hill of Tara one day he ran into, there being no better phrase to use, Laoighaire, the High King. Patrick had been going around the area where the king's palace was when a fight between the two men seemed on the cards. With such a relatively small band of followers, Patrick seemed to be on a hiding to nothing for he had certainly annoyed the king and incurred his mighty wrath. But he put his faith in God and somehow or other, with his powers of persuasion and Christian zeal, he managed to calm the king down and actually succeeded in converting him.

During these years Patrick encountered other important personages throughout the land. He met the king of Connaught in county Roscommon and travelled to many places in counties Sligo, Mayo and Donegal. It is also said that he even visited the Giant's Causeway, a place so beloved of the Irish to this day. He even sailed across to Caher Island off the Mayo coast and to the islands in Lough Corrib. It is really hard to imagine how difficult it would have been to find boats to take them over to these islands. But his determination shone through whether they were sailing on the high seas or climbing some of the highest mountains in the country.

To us today we can hardly believe that this could have happened, but it did and throughout his travels he was able to convert many more of the Irish lords and kings to the way of Christ. His belief in the power of prayer saved the day on many occasions for his little group.

Trials and tribulations for the blessed Patrick

Despite his success in converting the Irish, Patrick still had his demons to overcome. He was often tempted by being offered bribes, but he never yielded; he felt that his lack of education as a young man was a disadvantage, but he pressed on; he was often obstructed by people, but he simply ignored them and moved on; he never denied wrong doing knowing that God would forgive him.

There is no doubt, however, that the blessed Patrick was a good and worthy man in what was still a wicked and ungodly world. And in Ireland he made Christianity a religion for all, the young, the brave and the gallant. He was, in today's parlance, a veritable Pied Piper. He focussed on his goal to convert the Irish and in this endeavour he was hugely successful.

The death of Saint Patrick

It is generally acknowledged that Patrick died in the year 461AD at Saul and probably on 17 March. He would have been in his middle 70s. The question is still asked to this day – where was he buried? There are those in Armagh, Ireland's primatial see, who assert that he is buried there. But the best information we have, perhaps by reading into what he himself said in his Confessio that, whilst at one time he did want to be buried in Armagh, he decided in the end that he wanted to return to the area where he first came – and that was Downpatrick which is close to his arrival point at Saul. And so it is that a stone is placed close to the Cathedral of the Holy Trinity, Down, in Downpatrick, which represents not the actual place of burial, but a focal point where visitors and pilgrims to the cathedral can stand and pray – and thank God for sending such a wonderful and holy man to Ireland in the fifth century. It should be noted too that also buried on the Hill of Down where the cathedral stands, are the remains of Ireland's other two greatest saints, St Brigid and St Columcille (or Columba). This surely places Downpatrick as the single most holy place in the whole of Ireland.

Patrick's wells and mountains

But the good people of Downpatrick must not forget that Patrick, whilst laid to rest there, travelled throughout the island and in almost any town and village in most parts of Ireland are to be found shrines and wells commemorating our beloved patron saint. There are, as could be easily imagined, places of pilgrimage in the Downpatrick area. There are wells, for example, at Mearne, near Saul, at Struell, in the same vicinity and at Raholp a few miles from Downpatrick. There is a very fine well on the island of Inchagoill in Lough Corrib, county Mayo, another at Navan in county Armagh and one at Clebagh in county Roscommon.

The two mountains most associated with Patrick are Slemish (438m) in county Antrim, the site of his early days as a slave shepherd, and Croagh Patrick (762m) in county Mayo. One would think that pilgrims would regularly visit both these holy mountains. This is the case with Croagh Patrick where Patrick is reputed to have fasted forty days and forty nights during his travels. Every year thousands of pilgrims from every part of Ireland and further afield come to climb this holy mountain, most of them completing the difficult climb barefoot, and praying at the church built at the summit. The exact opposite, however, is the case with Slemish – it is rarely, if ever, climbed by pilgrims and only perhaps by a few intrepid mountain climbers. There is never any discussion as to the reason for the total neglect of Slemish as compared with the popularity of Croagh Patrick. Perhaps it is simply because that the saint's days on Slemish when he was a slave boy minding his master's sheep were considered much less significant compared with his latter days when he doing God's work Christianising the Irish.

Many people ask whether there still are any churches from the period. There are none for they were built of wood and would have fallen into disrepair and vanished many centuries ago. There are replicas of the type of building of the time not least the present Church of Ireland church of St Patrick at Saul, which is now built in the style of an ancient place of worship.

Do we have anything written by Patrick himself?
The straightforward answer is yes we do. The only words that we still have are contained in his Confessio, his confession, and his Letter to the soldiers of Coroticus. These documents make interesting reading for everyone and for scholars of the patron saint they are blessed gems. Much has, of course, been written over the centuries about this great and Christian man and perhaps the best way to conclude this story is to quote these beautiful words –

'A righteous man verily was this man, with purity like the patriarchs.

A true pilgrim like Abraham.

Mild, forgiving from the heart like Moses.

A praiseworthy psalmist like David.

A student of wisdom like Solomon.

A choice vessel for proclaiming righteousness like Paul the apostle.

A man full of the grace and of the favour of the Holy Spirit like John the child.

A fair herb garden with plants of virtues.

A vine branch of fruitfulness.

A flashing fire with the fervour of the warming and heating of the sons of Life, for kindling and inflaming charity.

A lion through strength and might.

A dove for gentleness and simplicity.

A serpent for prudence and cunning as to good.

Gentle, humble, merciful unto the sons of Life.

Gloomy, ungentle to the sons of Death.

A laborious and serviceable slave to Christ.

A king for dignity and power as to binding and loosing, as to liberating and enslaving, as to killing and giving life.'

Saint Patrick may never have really loved the Irish but they loved and respected him, as is, of course, the case to this day.

Curious for more?

I can recommend these books for further reading:

Gallico, Paul, *The Steadfast Man – a Life of St. Patrick*, London, Michael Joseph Ltd., 1958.

McHugh, Michael. J., *Saint Patrick – Pioneer Missionary to Ireland*, Illinois, Christian Liberty Press, 1999.

For books that aren't in common circulation I may be able to source them for you. Email me at clive.scoular@gmail.com or check out my website – *clivescoular.com*.

The Stolen Village

An Irish story of kidnapping and enslavement

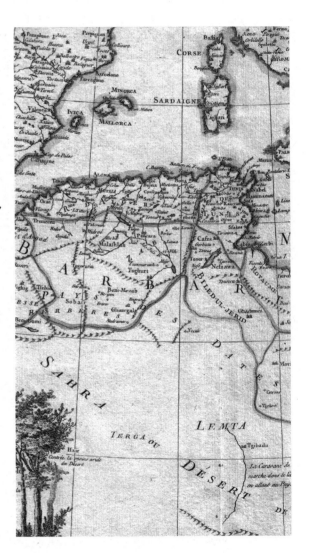

Map of 17th century north Africa

IN JUNE 1631, a pirate ship from north Africa attacked a little Irish village and stole over 100 of its people. But this is Ireland. How and why could such a thing have happened? This tragic story will now enfold just to prove that there did exist scheming pirates hell bent on disrupting even a sleepy little settlement on the south coast of Ireland – and in the early years of the seventeenth century.

The sleepy village of Baltimore in county Cork

In 1631 Baltimore was but a small community of a few hundred inhabitants, most of whose ancestors had arrived from England in the previous century. As a consequence there were a fair number of Calvinists and evangelical Anglicans living there. The lands in that part of county Cork had once belonged to the O'Driscolls but they had been driven out from what they had hoped would be their stronghold for many centuries. Baltimore had fallen on hard times but was, at last, slowly recovering. Unsurprisingly, for a small coastal village, many of the folk who lived there were fishermen and their womenfolk worked in the associated fish sheds on the piers beside Roaring Water Bay. It was a hard life but one which suited these honest souls.

And so the story unfolds

During the early hours of 20 June 1631, over 200 corsairs, or pirates, sailed into Roaring Water Bay close to the village of Baltimore.

Everyone was fast asleep when the attackers landed on the shore and they immediately set about burning the homes of the innocent inhabitants. The terrified men, women and children rushed out of their houses straight into the arms of their assailants. To use the word 'terrified' would have been an understatement as they stared into the eyes of these Janissaries, to give them their proper title. They were dressed in exotic red uniforms, with colourful turbans and baggy pants. And they carried in their hands their fierce implement of war, the yatagan, a broad bladed sword designed to instil terror in whoever stood in front of them.

As the frightened families ran out, they had nowhere to go. They could fight or flee but the two men of the village who did try to resist were ruthlessly slaughtered in front of their own families and neighbours. The leader of this gang of kidnappers was a man called Morat Rais, a very experienced man who had been involved in piracy for many years. This may have been the first time an Irish village had been invaded like this but for Morat and his men attacking villages like this was almost an everyday occurrence.

As the victims were rounded up in the lower part of the village, Morat and his men considered that they could also attack the upper part of Baltimore. But, before his men could turn their attention to this further onslaught, some of the men of Baltimore raised the alarm, started setting fires and banging drums and all this to ensure that the villagers who remained had some time to effect an escape if need be. Consequently Morat decided that, rather than jeopardise his plans and the safety of his men, he would cut his losses and leave. After all he did have a large number of fit and healthy prospective slaves in his custody and so, without further ado, he corralled them into their stinking little boats at the shore and rowed them out to his ship moored in the bay. Once aboard he could assess his haul – 23 men, 34 women and 50 youngsters. Probably the greatest heartbreak in the midst of this tragedy was the fact that the seven sons of William Gunter were taken in the raid though not William himself. Within a short time the ship carrying these unfortunates was fast moving away from land and out into the sea routes to a place unknown – what was their destination and, when they did have a moment to reflect on their utter misfortune, would they ever see their homes again?

Who was Morat Rais?
The attack on Baltimore might have been the first raid on Irish soil but piracy and kidnapping were common occurrences in those days. There were many ships sailing up and down the English coast raiding places on shore and capturing little ships as they sailed by. These boats were attacked, their crews kidnapped and their cargoes stolen before the ships themselves were sunk. It was a dangerous occupation to be an ordinary sailor in those days. These were the terrors of sailing the oceans in the early years of the seventeenth century.

Morat had sailed from Algiers in north Africa where he had been involved in such nefarious activities for years. He was already a man in his late fifties or early sixties and he evidently knew his trade. At one stage in his life, however, he had actually been a slave himself but he was able to escape and turn to piracy. He was skilled in mastering large ships as well as smaller ones, which were more effective as pirate ships. Believe it or not, Morat had once sailed to an island off the coast of Iceland in 1627 and taken 242 captives, leaving behind a scene of abject horror. Even to this very day, the Icelandic people still talk about this episode in their country's past. Morat lived near Algiers and by this stage he was a very rich man. He could have lived off his ill-gotten gains but chose to continue with the trade he knew best – capturing innocents and making them slaves.

Why then did he choose to attack Baltimore? Word had got out that an Irish port could be attacked – perhaps Kinsale or Cork itself. Morat saw an opportunity in such a venture and he had an English captain friend called Edward Fawlett who suggested that the small village of Baltimore would be a most suitable target. Morat also knew that he had to be careful about trusting people. But he set out from Algiers with southern Ireland in mind. He crewed the two ships he intended to take with men he thought he could trust. He was fairly happy with his men and, as was usual, they captured a number of small ships on the way to Ireland. This meant that, even before arriving there, he already had a number of healthy and fit slaves on board. Close to his destination, he boarded a small fishing vessel and discovered that its captain, one Hackett, knew more about Baltimore. He was assured that he would find plenty of suitable men, women and even children who would make ideal slaves back in Algiers. The assistance given by both Fawlett and Hackett stood Morat in good stead. So the scene was set. Baltimore had become the focus of his dastardly plan.

As far as Baltimore was concerned, the die was cast – completely unknown to the people of the village of course. Within a couple of hours on that fateful night, the little county Cork village was raided and enslaved. The journey to Africa for those devastated by this unthinkable and unmitigated disaster had begun.

Where are we going? Will this journey ever end? Will no one come to our aid?

This was a voyage to slavery; it was a journey to a place the unfortunates had never heard of; it was to be a part of their lives which would forever leave them feeling lonely, unloved and forgotten. Hopelessness and utter despondency reigned. They couldn't sleep aboard the filthy and stinking vessel because of the deplorable conditions below deck and the infestation of rats and insects. For the next month and a half they had to endure insufficient food, scraps and leftovers from the pirates' plates, putrid water and the fact that they never had any change of clothes. At least most of them were allowed on deck during the day where they at least were able to breathe fresh air and, whilst on deck, they could only watch with fascination the prayer rituals of the exotically dressed Janissaries. The captives participated in the entertainment put on by the pirates and the ship's crew and even sang some of their songs from home. As time passed by, captives and captors, whilst not exactly becoming friends, learned to tolerate one another.

In the early days of captivity some of the Baltimore people thought that someone would surely have heard of their plight and come to their aid. They were to be cruelly disappointed. No Royal Navy ships went in pursuit of Morat and his sailors and no local fishermen set out to try to help either for, with so many stories of piracy and kidnapping, none of them would dare to follow lest they too fell victim to the pirate ships. It seems that King Charles was told of the sack of Baltimore and went into a rage demanding information about those who had allowed such a thing to happen. But no one came to their assistance and the ship ploughed on towards its destination.

The captives asked where they were being taken and one of the crew told them about Algiers. The name and place of course meant absolutely nothing to any of them but, as the time went on, they did begin to find out more about this city on the north African coast. They were apprehensive, yet strangely inquisitive. In the last days of July, six weeks after leaving their Irish home, the captives entered Algiers harbour. The sailors were ecstatic for they had come home; for the men, women and children from Baltimore it was an altogether different sensation, a mixture of fear and trepidation, of dismay and alarm, but also of wonderment and amazement.

Arrival in Algiers

Grim reality soon struck home for the despondent captives. The men were taken below and shackled and the women and children were herded together in tightly knit groups. As they stared out from the decks of their prison ship, they witnessed a scene which they could never have imagined. Being used to their quiet Irish fishing village with its sweeping hills and lovely shorelines, they now gazed upon a thriving and bustling city. Even at first glance they saw people from every race and nation, from Africa and Europe and from Asia and the Americas. At the time they did not, of course, know exactly who everyone was, but they were soon to find out. Algiers had the most magnificent waterfront. They were later to discover that it had been built over the years by thousands of slaves from all over the world, many of whom had died during its construction. They soon began to realise that they too could soon be put to some such similar cruel task.

As they were led off the boat, cheering crowds welcomed the sailors on their return. These same crowds then turned towards the captives and jeered. The Baltimore folk were just the latest contingent of slaves to arrive in the city, and a very small group at that. Between 1621 and 1627, over 20,000 slaves had been brought into Algiers and so another 107 constituted but a miniscule addition to that number.

It is hard to believe that the English consul in the city actually came to meet the ship and so the captives hoped that something might possibly be done for them, but they were to be immediately disappointed. He could do nothing for them nor could he promise that ransoms might be paid for their release.

By now totally dejected and crestfallen, they were driven through the still taunting throngs to the royal palace. When they arrived, they could only stand in front of this fabulous edifice in astonishment and awe. It is impossible to imagine how and what they felt. The building was something they could never have dreamt of and they just wondered what would happen next.

The Pasha was a person to behold, dressed as he was in jewel-encrusted clothes and wearing a beautiful turban. The consul had come along with the captives in a further vain hope of appealing to the ruler's sense of decency and mercy. But he was quickly dismissed as the captives were lined up in front of the top man. They were checked up and down and made to feel even more miserable than they already were. Those the Pasha wanted, he took for his harem and the rest were simply taken to the slave market to be auctioned. Reality now began to sink in; their future was mapped out for them; they could only wonder what would become of them now.

An auction in a slave market

The remainder of the Baltimore captives were then driven to the slave market. Even worse, most of them were then separated from their own family members and suddenly realised that they would never see their loved ones again. This was the most awful moment for them; sons and daughters taken from their parents and husbands and wives from their spouses.

The women were dealt with first of all. Those not already acquired by the Pasha became servants and nurses if they were lucky, whilst the rest simply became playthings for their unscrupulous captors. There was no compassion shown as the women and girls were examined as if they were beasts for sale. Many of them found their way into harems and, whilst some of their masters were decent and kind, many were cruel, wicked and vile. And we also must remember that the Baltimore women were but a very small and insignificant percentage of the thousands of captive women in the city at any one time. It happened that many slave women, and this may have included some of those from Baltimore, bore children to sultans and rulers not just in Algiers but also throughout the entire Mediterranean region. Some actually became quite powerful women in their own right and others, incredible as it may seem, found true love. Others became companions to wealthy women and yet more learnt domestic skills like embroidery and needlework which enabled them to sell their goods and make a little bit of money. As time went on, the womenfolk settled down as best they could, many of them converting to Islam and marrying some of the local men. In their quieter moments, some of them even preferred living in these sunny climes than enduring their earlier existence in the boggy fields and often wet conditions in county Cork – perhaps life in Algiers was quite tolerable after all, despite the anguish of capture and separation.

Life for the captive men was a different matter. It was tougher and utterly merciless. One or two of the Baltimore men were condemned to a life as a galley slave. This meant that they were shackled with four others on a bench in a galley ship. They were quite cruelly treated and had nowhere to lay their heads and nowhere to eat their frugal fare, except on that very same bench. Their life was a misery and it is a miracle that any of them survived. Others were confined to filthy prison cells and made to undertake heavy work, day in and day out, regardless of the searing heat of the midday sun. Yet more were made to work on farms and quarries and were used as beasts of burden, being harnessed into ploughs like the horses and cattle they replaced.

But for some of the men there were stories and examples of better treatment from their captors. Some of their slave masters were quite enlightened and gave their slaves the opportunity to earn some money. Some of these men set up small craft businesses and even prospered. They were then able to save enough eventually to pay the ransom so that they could be freed. However, as far as the Baltimore men are concerned, there is no definite evidence that any of them managed to avail of this possibility. And there was little or no chance to escape; their future was clearly laid out before them; they would remain a slave, in whatever circumstance they found themselves.

For the children and young people amongst the Baltimore captives, life was quite tolerable. Boys from northern countries, like the British Isles, were considered highly prized and were treated well. There were some examples, however, of lads spending a very miserable childhood at the hands of cruel and wicked men. But it is fairly certain that none of the Irish boys suffered this fate. The girls were often taken as maidservants or as part of a harem and some went on to become rulers' wives as the years passed by. And, for most of the young people, they really had forgotten what life had been like in Ireland and had never any desire to return. It had become nothing more than an unknown land.

What of life back in Ireland? Would a ransom ever be paid?
There were recriminations back in county Cork in the weeks and months following the raid. The captain of the lone Royal Navy vessel which had been in the vicinity, and which had not even put to sea to try to prevent the tragedy, was simply admonished and the matter evidently clearly fudged and shelved. No one accepted responsibility and that seemed to be that. However the fishing boat captain, Hackett, who had helped Morat, was brought to court, found guilty and put to death in Cork.

Then the question was asked, especially by those relatives of the captives still living in Baltimore – would anyone put up the money for a ransom to be paid? The local gentry, including the Earl of Cork, could probably have funded such an operation but declined to do so. Other well-meaning people in the area did talk about helping the unfortunates but nothing came of any of their endeavours. The consul in Algiers repeatedly appealed to the King and Privy Council in London but without much success. Occasionally one or two captives from the British Isles were freed on payment of a ransom and, in 1646, fifteen years after the incident, two of the Baltimore women were set free. But for the remaining 105 captives they were on their own and they realised that there was little chance of being repatriated. Their hopes were, however, raised when a ship arrived from England to negotiate but nothing came of this attempt to return them to their homeland. Back in Algiers the Baltimore folk just had to get on with their lives as best they could. The young people forgot about their homeland; the women folk got on with their lives with the local men; the men slaved away.

County Cork had forgotten their enslaved friends and relatives and got on with their lives too.

A real surprise, a successful escape

The Baltimore captives, after all these years in Algiers, did what they could to make their lives as tolerable as possible. Some still had difficulty in finding enough food to survive and they had to live by their wits. This was oft times dangerous as, if they had been caught stealing food for example, they would have been dealt with severely by their lords and masters. There were, however, advantages to living in Algiers. It was a modern place with fine buildings and good services. There were doctors who were skilled in their profession and their whole surroundings were healthy. Looking back the Baltimore folk began to understand that life in Algiers, even as a slave, was a safer, brighter and more comfortable place to live than in their homes in county Cork.

It has been noted that the prospect of escaping the clutches of the hierarchy in Algiers was slim, to say the least. But one small group of men proved that it was possible, given a favourable wind so to speak. An Anglican clergyman, the Reverend Devereux Spratt, who had been a slave himself until he was freed, had decided to stay in Algiers and minister to his small congregation. He soon involved himself in a plan to assist five English slaves to escape. None of the Baltimore men were part of this scheme but would have heard about it.

The leader of the escape group was a man called William Oakley. He had a business in the city making waterproof canvas clothes and he was determined to use his skills to build a canvas boat. He had the materials and the drive to go ahead with this plan, which he realised was going to be very risky. He arranged that there should be thrice weekly gospel and prayer meetings in one of the storerooms in his premises. This meant that, whilst he and his associates were hammering and building their boat, he knew that any sounds they were making would not be heard above the lusty singing of the congregation. This ploy worked well and he had his vessel ready for launching in double quick time. After one of the meetings, the five men, with Oakley in charge, lifted their boat down to the water's edge and got away without any of the guards seeing them. They had a most perilous voyage across the Mediterranean and eventually arrived, exhausted but safe, on the shores of the island of Majorca. This was a daring deed although it was probably the only such venture to succeed. Back in Algiers, the authorities were cursing themselves for having let such an escape happen and, when they found out that the Reverend Spratt had known about it, they severely grilled him and most thought that he would be put to death. But amazingly he was allowed to leave the country and returned to England. In his later years he became the rector of the parish church in Mitchelstown in county Cork where he served for the rest of his life. To this day a plaque can be seen in the church reminding visitors and locals alike of the story of this remarkable, and truly lucky, man.

What did happen to the Baltimore folk? And what of Morat Rais?

All we really have is measured guesswork. Only two of the women were freed as we have noted. The remainder of the Baltimore people would have spent the rest of their lives in the circumstances already described. They would have grown old in their new surroundings often with families of their own born to them and their African husbands as the years went by. They had been completely forgotten back in Ireland and none would have been able to return, even if they wanted it. And anyway, who would want to return to rain soaked Baltimore from sunny Algiers?

As for Morat, he was captured in later years by corsairs but managed to escape. He lived to a ripe old age in a fine castle. As he looked back on his life as a pirate, he might not even have remembered the episode of his kidnapping of the Baltimore 107. How many people in west county Cork or anywhere in Ireland for that matter know anything about that fateful day in June 1631 when burning and devastation hit this lovely corner of Ireland, with so many of its inhabitants taken into slavery? The answer is that very few people know of this tragedy although there do exist one or two reminders of this story in Baltimore itself.

Curious for more?

I can recommend this book for further reading:

Ekin, Des, *The Stolen Village – Baltimore and the Barbary Pirates*, Dublin, O'Brien Press, 2006.

For books that aren't in common circulation I may be able to source them for you. Email me at clive.scoular@gmail.com or check out my website – *clivescoular.com*.

The Famine Years

1845 – 1849

Bridget O'Donnell and her children, West Cork

THE IRISH WERE light hearted, happy, hospitable and well mannered. They might have been wretched but they were healthy and full of fun. They were taller and more robust than their neighbours across the Irish Sea and they lived longer than most of the people in other western European countries. They lived, on average, for 37 or 38 years, which was at the high end of life expectancy in the mid nineteenth century. They grew to the dizzy heights of 5 feet 7 inches which was almost unheard of in any other part of the United Kingdom. They married young and produced large families although many of their children did die young – a fate which also sadly befell many generations of British children.

But what made the Irish so good-looking and handsome and the envy of the rest of Europe? What produced these athletic men and beautiful women? The answer is simple, if indeed hard to comprehend. It was the potato. We know that the potato contained more good and nutritious ingredients than did any other foodstuff. In that simple item were to be found starch, sugar, nitrogen, vitamin C and a host of other wholesome minerals.

The Irish, although decidedly poor, did have other advantages. Their homes were warm, if small and often windowless, and their workplace was just ten feet from the door of their cottage; their fields of potatoes, though small as well, were literally on their doorsteps.

However despite these positive points about the Irish we all know that the great famine struck in 1845. For the Irish, and actually for other European peoples, a famine was not at all uncommon. Most thought that the pestilence would only last a year or so like many of the previous ones and that they would just about manage to survive. There had been regular famines over the past century and the years 1740 to 1741, just over one hundred years earlier, had brought a most devastating famine. At that time the population of the country was just a little over two million and, in just that single year, one sixth (around 350,000) of its people died. During the early years of the nineteenth century too there had been yet more famines. So Ireland was never immune and the famine to hit in 1845 seemed just like any other and would probably be over relatively soon. By the summer of 1847, which was a wonderfully warm and pleasant one, the Irish truly believed that the pestilence had finally passed. But the blight hit even harder as the year, known as 'Black 47', progressed offering no respite for a dying nation. By the fourth year, 1848, over a million of the population had died of disease and starvation and two million had emigrated.

During 1849 there was even a visit by Queen Victoria to Ireland and, rather than being rebuked for coming during such a difficult time, she was welcomed with open arms. Who said the Irish were an ungracious people? It really was not until 1850 that the horror had ended. There were, in truth, not many healthy people left, and yet as the 1850s progressed, the nation's recovery to good health was spectacular. Those who had survived managed to find more potatoes to plant and, for some years henceforward, the population numbers bounced back in a miraculous fashion. The potato was proving its worth once more although in the back of everyone's mind was that clawing thought – when will another famine hit our fair and pleasant land?

Why such a dependence on the potato?

We have seen what a wonderfully nutritious food the potato was – and still is. But why the total dependence on it? Prior to the arrival of the potato in Ireland in the early years of the eighteenth century, the average Irish family ate vegetables, bread, offal and perhaps a pig at Christmas time. Then the potato took over. It was easy to grow and required just a small patch to provide enough to feed a family for almost an entire year. The crop was sown and then all that had to be done was to tend the potato patch and harvest it at the appropriate time. Irish families only ever needed a good-sized pot in which to boil their potatoes and day-by-day they enjoyed eating their filling meals perhaps accompanied, if they were lucky, by a little buttermilk. In fact a man often ate over 15 pounds each and every day and, as long as there were potatoes, his family grew stronger by the day. It is true to say that from June to August, when the stock of potatoes had run out, the families would have gone hungry, but they always knew that, by September, the new crop would be ready to feed them for most of the following year.

Dependence meant that the average peasant Irishman and woman had forgotten how to do anything other than boil a pot of water to cook their sole meal. They had lost the art of baking bread and cooking different types of meals; they no longer bothered to plant other vegetables and they had, even if they lived by the sea, disregarded any need to go out and catch fish. In truth these folk had gone to sea to catch fish in little smacks but most of these had been destroyed in the Great Wind and storms a few years before the famine in 1839. Thus the potato dominated life in the Irish homestead. Even in the Big Houses, whilst there was never a total reliance on the potato, a great many of their meals consisted solely of the wonder crop.

However there was always another crop being grown in the gardens of the Irish peasant farmer. He may have been concentrating on caring for his wholesome potatoes, but he was also growing grain. The reason for this was not of course to use this as an alternative food source - it was to pay his rent. The landlord expected payment and received it in this form. The Irishman knew how to plant and harvest it but had no idea what to do with it. The grain was taken into the landlords' barns and exported from Ireland in vast quantities. The question is always asked – why was so much food exported from a starving Ireland when it could have been used to feed its dying people? But it was of little use to the Irish – they didn't know what to do with it and anyway they had their potatoes.

Was there any help for the starving Irish?
There was a little assistance coming from the government in the early days of the famine. Indian corn was brought in by ship and distributed throughout the bigger concentrations of the population but, although it was a source of sustenance, it proved a very difficult food to prepare and eat. It needed a very strong kind of implement to crush it in readiness for making a meal and very few of the poor possessed it. Consequently few, if any, of the population benefitted

from Indian meal. If there had been a few vegetables available they were quickly consumed and rarely replanted. In fact, as the famine gripped the land over these years, many of the starving people had to resort to eating weeds from their gardens and the roadside.

The real help came from those beneficent and kindly Quakers who came over from England and set up soup kitchens. At the outset these proved to be an absolute Godsend and as many as three million people were fed by these and similar generous people. In the early days, however, it was more difficult to get these kitchens to country locations which made life even more desperate for those living in the west of Ireland for example. Soup kitchens did spring up in situations like the famine and kept many starving people alive. But as the years passed by the quality of the soup deteriorated. Some would ask why and the answer is because wholesome ingredients were in short supply, which resulted in the soup becoming too watery, thus doing more harm than good. It simply ran through the recipient and caused more problems than it solved. But to give credit where it is due, the Irish would surely have died in even greater numbers had it not been for the generosity and hard work of the Quakers.

In general terms the government did not help. To begin with they reminded people that the famine had hit Great Britain as well as Ireland, although the Scots, Welsh and English did have alternative foodstuffs and household skills to avert a disaster. Secondly they considered that the famine would, in all likelihood, last just for one year going by previous experiences. Thirdly the Prime Ministers of those days, Robert Peel and Lord John Russell, were stern individuals and probably not very caring and their man in Ireland at the time,

Charles Trevelyan, Christian gentleman though he undoubtedly was, became the virtual dictator of Irish relief. Therefore it is clear to see that not much was going for the poor Irish.

Disease as well as starvation

Many people, who only have a scant knowledge of the Great Irish Famine, assume that the famine deaths were caused solely by starvation and this is a very reasonable assumption. Famine equals lack of food and therefore the outcome must lead to death. But the reality is far from this supposition. When people begin to starve and have to hunt for food, the inevitable outcome is that they are struck down by virulent and life threatening diseases. They no longer have any defence against disease and they become easy prey to the myriad of sicknesses lying in wait for them. It was to cruelly prove that the vast majority of this vulnerable and helpless people died from disease and not from starvation.

The first disease to strike was land scurvy. Most of us have heard of scurvy but we tend to associate this with sailors aboard ship. But this strain, caused by the complete lack of vitamin C which had been found in healthy potatoes, was a horrible virus which was louse borne and led to swollen limbs accompanied by scratching and a foul smell. Other louse borne diseases were typhus and relapsing fever and probably the most distressing condition was epidemic fever which indiscriminately skipped through all the social classes meaning that even those doctors, clergy and nurses who were helping the poor were infected themselves and died in great numbers too. As the famine years progressed dysentery and smallpox (which had been eliminated from Ireland in the early part of the century) carried off many of the people who had resorted to eating scratchings and weeds from the roadsides. These poor Irishmen and women had no resistance whatsoever and were dying from this catalogue of diseases in their tens of thousands. About the only disease not to afflict the Irish was cholera which was never present in those years, but this was hardly what might be considered as a positive amidst the horrors of the famine.

The workhouses and outdoor relief

By the beginning of the famine in 1845 Ireland had 130 workhouses. These buildings, which eventually numbered over 160, were built throughout the entire island of Ireland in or close to all the centres of population. They were constructed to a simple, yet sturdy, design and were to provide for the needs of the most unfortunate members of society. They were staffed by men and women whose job it was to care for those entering their domain, but not to overindulge them or to feed them with anything other than basic food. This was a deliberate policy to make the workhouses rather unattractive so that only those who were desperate would look for this accommodation. But the fact that these places of refuge were available when the famine broke out did prove to be a lifesaver for many of the poor and hungry Irish. By the middle years of the famine these workhouses were full to overflowing and some even had to erect tents or take over neighbouring houses to meet the ever-increasing demands. Many of these workhouses remain in use to this day, many of them still providing care services for those of the present day generation.

As the famine progressed government introduced what they called outdoor relief. Jobs were made available and, although as many as three quarters of a million were working on these schemes by 1847, fewer and fewer of the men employed were fit and able enough to continue – they were just too ill and hungry. Those who were able to continue earned the miserly sum of between 8d (4p) and 2/- (10p) per week. The schemes had to be paid for by the Irish themselves which, to all intents and purposes, defeated the whole raison d'etre for relief. And yet many roads and piers, for example, were built making Ireland the country with the most paved roads per square mile in the entire continent of Europe.

At the same time during these dreadful years, the railways of Ireland were being constructed and, between 1845 and 1850, the total miles of track increased from 70 to 700. Even in the worst hit part of the country, in county Cork, the railway from Cork to Bandon and on into county Kerry was constructed. The men who built these railways were shipped in from Britain and very few of the starving Irish were involved. It is hard to think of the many railway workers being fed and clothed as they were building the railway whilst death from disease and starvation was being visited upon the poor peasant Irish all around them.

Emigration

Almost two million Irish men and women, and their children, left Ireland during and immediately following the years of the Great Famine. Emigration, however, was not a new phenomenon. In the thirty years before the famine, from 1815 until 1845, one million

Irish had emigrated. These were mainly poor Roman Catholics who realised that their chances of making a better life for themselves and their families no longer lay in Ireland but in the New World of Canada and America. Some even made their new homes in Great Britain and the boats sailing from eastern Irish ports to places like Liverpool overflowed with fleeing Irish. Ireland, to so many, might be a wonderful place but unfortunately no longer a country to rear their families.

In the latter half of the eighteenth century there was another mass emigration from Ireland. This time the relatively well off northern Presbyterians were leaving in their droves, chased out by an oppressive Anglican Church which penalised these their fellow Protestants just as much as it did the majority Roman Catholic population. The 'down trodden' of Ireland were not just the Roman Catholics but everyone else, Presbyterian, Methodist, Congregationalist and Jew, all those who were not members of the Established Church. This earlier emigration proved a great benefit to the burgeoning American nation for, in succeeding years, these northern Protestants became the legislators and Presidents of that emerging country.

Travelling to north America for the starving Irish was, of course, a very different matter. Many of them did have support from their landlords who encouraged them to leave for a better future and provided the necessary funds for them to make the journey. Much is often said about the wicked and uncaring gentry who evicted their tenants and forced them on to so called 'coffin' ships to take their chances to reach America. Some of these stories are true but we must never tar all landlords with the one cruel and uncaring brush.

The decision to emigrate was a hard one to make. Those who wanted to leave had to take many points into consideration. Were they fit enough? Could they afford the cost of the journey? Did they really want to leave their homeland? Many of them lived miles from the nearest port, be it Cork, Dublin, Londonderry or even Sligo and other small ports in the west of Ireland. If they made it to the place of embarkation, they had to find a ship and they had to pay their fare. The fare to Canada was £4 and to America, £6. Most initially wanted to go to America but it was decidedly more difficult to be admitted there, especially if they were ill or suffering from disease. It was easier to go to Canada but the wait on board ship in the St Lawrence river to be examined at the admitting stations on Grosse Ile proved difficult. Many of the ships which eventually reached Canada had been at sea for perhaps as many as fourteen weeks and, by the time they reached their destination, many of the emigrants had died on board. Those who survived then had this long and tortuous wait to be examined and allowed to enter Canada. The reason for the majority of ships heading for Canada was the fact that this country was also part of the British Empire and therefore other British subjects were more easily admitted. Many thousands however never made it to either Canada or America. Even if they did not succumb on board ship, many others died as they waited to be examined on Grosse Ile. Those who did make it had to try to find lodgings in places like Montreal and other Canadian towns on the shores of the St Lawrence. And it was cold, very cold, in those cities. It is hard to believe that any of them ever actually survived their ordeal. In truth many Irish did colonise parts of French Canada but many of them did make it overland to America. It is almost impossible to imagine the journeys they had to make over many hundreds of miles to reach even the most northerly of the American states. Why then did they even try? To those who tackled the trek south, there was the hope, and expectation, of the green and pleasant land of their beloved America. They just had to get there – America was their destiny.

The cities of the American east coast may have beckoned but when the starving and emaciated Irish men and women eventually struggled into their midst, they were not made welcome. In fact they were ignored, sidelined and snubbed. They could not find accommodation except in the vilest parts of the ghettos of the cities; they could not get work except at the most menial tasks; they could not find friends apart from perhaps other Irish in the same miserable predicament. In a word, the despised Irish were beginning to wonder why they had come at all – was not America the Promised Land? For two long generations into the twentieth century the immigrant Irish had to suffer the ignominies of degradation and wretchedness. They tried to eke out an existence just to keep their little families alive and to remit some money to their impoverished relatives back in Ireland. But, in the end, the strength and determination of the Irish overcame their woes and they succeeded in making a name for themselves in all parts of American society. By the 1920s and 1930s it was the Irish who were running the cities which, just a few decades earlier, had disdainfully pretended that they had not existed.

And so the story of the Great Famine of the 1840s and its dreadful aftermath proved that, despite the deaths and emigration, the Irish could survive and then contribute to societies beyond their native land. Probably the most amazing statistic is that, within ten years of that disastrous pestilence, Ireland's population started to increase once again and they took their chances to carry on. One question does, however, remain. Did the Irish cease to depend on their blessed potato? The answer is 'not really'.

Curious for more?

I can recommend these books for further reading:

Keneally, Thomas, *The Great Shame*, UK, BCA, 1998.

Kerr, Donal A., *'A Nation of Beggars'? Priests, People, and Politics in Famine – Ireland 1846-1852*, Oxford, University Press, 1994.

Kinealy, Christine and Mac Atasney, Gerard, *The Hidden Famine – Hunger, Poverty and Sectarianism in Belfast*, London, Pluto Press, 2000.

Kinealy, Christine and Parkhill, Trevor, *The Famine in Ulster, Belfast*, Ulster Historical Foundation, 1997.

O Grada, Cormac, *The Great Irish Famine*, Dublin, Gill and Macmillan, 1989.

O Murchadha, Ciaran, *The Great Famine – Ireland's Agony – 1845-1852*, London, Bloomsbury, 2011.

Woodham-Smith, Cecil, *The Great Hunger*, New York, Harper and Row, 1963.

For books that aren't in common circulation I may be able to source them for you. Email me at clive.scoular@gmail.com or check out my website – *clivescoular.com*.

The Fremantle Mission

A daring rescue from the other side of the world

Escaped prisoners rowing towards the Catalpa

LIKE ALL STORIES concerning Ireland in the past two centuries, this tale is definitely one of daring and bravado and is, to all intents and purposes, one of the most exciting ever to be told.

In 1858 James Stephens formed an organisation called the Irish Republican Brotherhood – the IRB. Like so many Irishmen of his generation, he was determined that Ireland should be separate from the rest of the United Kingdom. He was prepared to use force and his IRB was set up with the utmost secrecy in mind. It was to be an oath-bound organisation which was not only against the law and punishable by severe penalties but was also in conflict with the Roman Catholic Church. This did not worry Stephens and he soon appointed 'circles' and 'centres' to ensure that those who were sworn members would only have contact with their own direct captains and colonels. He realised that previous rebellions and uprisings had been largely defeated not by any force of arms but by the deceit and treachery of paid informants.

Soon IRB branches spread throughout the country. Many of its members had been involved in other nefarious groupings which had failed in the past and so were determined that the IRB should succeed. The organisation attracted men from all classes and creeds and they soon started to prepare for their goal. They were in touch with Irish Americans to help them with the purchase of arms, the supply of money and help from their officers. The organisation similar to the IRB in America was called the Fenians and both groups were soon working in close cooperation with one another. Proof of how well they did work together was demonstrated in November 1861 when the body of an exiled Irishman, Terence McManus, was brought back from America for burial at Glasnevin in Dublin. It was the ideal opportunity for the new IRB to show how committed they were to their revolutionary goal. Presumably it must also have attracted the attention of the British authorities but no action was taken.

Stephens was clearly at the head of an organisation prepared to take on the British. By 1864 there were reputed to be 60,000 IRB men in Ireland with plenty of support from an even greater number of Fenians in America. It was time to move and preparations were begun to stage a rising in 1865.

The big plans soon begin to unravel

James Stephens was a man with a mission; he was at the head of a formidable force of men throughout Ireland; but did he have the bottle to push on? The answer was not really.

Although he clearly had a sophisticated organisation, Stephens was still heavily dependent on the Americans and when they suggested that an invasion of Canada by the Fenians would be more popular than a rising in Ireland, the first chinks in the armour began to appear. It is incredible to think that a few thousand republican Americans would even consider the enormity of invading their neighbour to the north. What could they have possibly achieved against the Canadians who had a strong military force of their own in every part of that huge dominion? But they did push into Canada in 1866 (and, as it happens, later again in 1870) with absolutely no hope of success and their incursions were unmitigated disasters. What was Stephens to do now to get his plans back on track?

British soldiers in the IRB

Whilst Stephens was what might be described as the titular head of the IRB, there was another very prominent and important man in the organisation upon whose shoulders rested much of the responsibility for running the IRB. This was John Devoy, born in Ireland in 1843, and a man who would dominate much of Irish revolutionary thinking from his American home for years to come.

It was Devoy who became the recruiter of IRB members within the British Army. By 1865 there were reckoned to be as many as 8,000 IRB men in the army in Ireland out of a total of 26,000. There were also many IRB soldiers in army bases in Great Britain as well. This meant that Devoy had a ready-made private army if a rising should ever come to pass. There were many able soldiers and outstanding 'centres'. Arrangements were therefore made, by some of the English 'circles', to seize a steamer, fill it with men and effect an invasion of Ireland. But this madcap scheme never came to pass.

Delays, arrests and failure

The rising was to take place, as has been already noted, in 1865. But it was postponed until March 1867. There were three main reasons for this apart, perhaps, from cold feet. The Americans were divided as to whether to come to Ireland or invade Canada. They invaded Canada which immediately meant that sufficient men and money were no longer forthcoming to assist the IRB. By the autumn of 1865 many of the Irish leaders, eventually including Stephens himself, had been arrested which, as a direct consequence of his postponing the rising, led to a demoralising of the rank and file. They had lost their drive and now that the British authorities had discovered what was happening within the army, the civilians in the IRB, who previously had been so enthusiastic, now kept their heads down and got on with their private lives.

Most of the leading lights in the IRB, including John Devoy, were arrested in February 1866 and some were sentenced to death, although these men had their punishments commuted. The following six men, who were to become the heroes of the story about to unfold, were sentenced to deportation to Australia following their courts martial: Thomas Darragh from county Wicklow, Thomas Hassett, Martin Hogan and Michael Harrington from county Cork, Robert Cranston from county Tyrone and James Wilson from Newry, county Down.

These men had given exemplary service in the army, although they had, like thousands of others, joined the IRB.

The story unfolds – transportation to Australia
In October 1867, 320 convicts and 63 IRB men were loaded aboard the *Hougoumont* for deportation to Western Australia. They were chained in iron fetters in preparation for a very long sea voyage of over 14,000 miles. The prospect was daunting although, once the ship sailed, the IRB men were reasonably well looked after by their guards who, like the IRB men themselves, had served in the British army.

We can only imagine the trials and tribulations of such a long sea journey which lasted for almost three months. Arriving at Fremantle, just south of Perth in Western Australia, the prisoners were quickly transferred from the ship to the 'Establishment' – the name of the convict prison in the little town. There were already over 1,000 prisoners incarcerated within its walls.

Fremantle was nothing more than a settlement when it was decided to build a convict prison there. Everything was centred around the prison and practically every building, bridge and road had been constructed by the prisoners over the years. Even the police stations, courthouses, the Town Hall and Government House had also been built by generations of convicts. But there would be no more prisoners coming to Fremantle. The complement aboard the *Hougoumont* was to be the last ship to arrive there laden with cheap labour. Transportation would soon be a thing of the past.

The locals, who were loyal to the Crown, were never happy with the constant arrival of prisoners and particularly despised IRB men. Within the prison, rules were harsh especially when the convicts had to work in the direct sunlight without any protection from the heat. Any free time they had, they spent writing letters home.

A new organisation formed in America – Clan na Gael

It is essential that we learn something of this new grouping in America for it was to be through their auspices that the six IRB men would be rescued.

The Clan na Gael, who were formerly the Fenians, were established in New York in 1867 by Jerome Collins who had come from Dunmanway in county Cork. Like its predecessor the Clan prospered and many clubs were set up all over the United States.

A number of the IRB leaders who had been imprisoned and later released on condition that they leave Ireland, came to live in America – amongst whom were John Devoy, Jeremiah Donovan Rossa and Thomas Luby. They joined the Clan upon their arrival but were unimpressed by the rituals and methods of running the organisation. So they set about trying to effect an amalgamation of both groups. In the end they succeeded, although it wasn't until 1875 that the final and agreed structure came into force. This clearly showed that the Irishmen were determined in their endeavour and to have joined up their respective groupings in such a relatively short time, was quite an achievement.

Amnesty for some, but not for others

Back in Britain a campaign to grant amnesties to IRB prisoners was gathering force and eventually came to fruition with their release in 1871. This included those in Fremantle who soon settled down in different parts of the country. However IRB prisoners who had been in the military were not included in the general release. This meant that the six men in Fremantle prison would not be able to avail of the amnesty and they soon appealed to their friends in the IRB to make the government change its mind – but without success.

John Devoy took up the baton to do something for the men left in Fremantle prison. But he did not receive much support from his friends in the Clan. He was being sent letters regularly from the Fremantle men who even told him that the other IRB men who had been released had completely abandoned them. If someone didn't do something soon, they would remain prisoners until their dying day. James Wilson decided to write to Devoy with a credible plan for escape. If a whaler could be sent for them then they could make plans. But something would have to be done soon as some of the men were increasingly unwell. It was a case of 'now or never'.

A plan to rescue the men

Devoy and some of his friends worked out a plan and brought it to the Baltimore Clan Convention in 1874. They needed to convince the 'big wigs' on the committee that their plan had a fair chance of success provided that the members supported it. This was going to be a tricky endeavour especially as they would need to divulge their plot to the entire organisation. The membership supported Devoy and it is remarkable that secrecy was upheld. They had been given the approval of the Clan – now they had to put their plan into practice. It was going to be difficult but the thought of their friends rotting in a Western Australian jail spurred them on.

They needed to know something about the gaol and how an escape could be implemented and this precious information was given to them by men who had just been released from the prison. Their first hurdle had been overcome. Now they needed to raise funds to buy a ship. With just $7,000 raised they knew their only option was to put the prisoners aboard a whaler, which would have called at Fremantle. But this was not a wise plan for they did not know if they could trust the ship's captain. Devoy decided to go to see Captain Henry Hathaway in the port of New Bedford in Massachusetts to seek his advice. He recommended that a whaler of their own should be bought and it could partly pay its way by catching some whales on the voyage which would help defray the expenses. This seemed a very sound idea and so Devoy determined to raise more money. He soon raised $12,000 which would enable the plan to proceed.

Buying a ship and making the arrangements for the voyage

Captain Hathaway quickly located a suitable vessel and Devoy went to purchase it at New Bedford. But it had been already sold by the time he arrived. Luckily it was not long until they found, and bought, the *Catalpa* on 27 April 1875. They were also pleased that its captain, George Anthony, was prepared to sail the ship and accordingly he was taken into the confidence of the Clan men. It turned out that Anthony's appointment was an inspired choice. A number of alterations were made to the *Catalpa* but, in so doing, the costs went up and by the time it was ready, the *Catalpa* had cost $19,000. Nevertheless Devoy did find the necessary additional funds and the ship was ready to sail.

Before the ship could leave, however, other vital plans had to be made. It was decided that two men, John Breslin and Tom Desmond, should be sent to Fremantle in advance to make contact with the prisoners and help with preparations for the rescue. Devoy wanted to be one of these men but he was discouraged as it was felt that he was needed at home. He reluctantly agreed and the two men chosen set off for San Francisco where they boarded a ship going to Sydney. This journey took a little over a month and once there they quickly discovered that the Australian IRB already had a plan to rescue the prisoners. This could easily have caused problems for Breslin and Desmond but fortunately the Australians agreed to cooperate with them and put their funds at their disposal. They then set sail for Western Australia and arrived at Fremantle by the middle of November 1875. The scene was set. The Clan representatives were in Fremantle; the prisoners had been contacted and the *Catalpa* had set sail to effect their rescue. But would the plan work out? Only time would tell.

The voyage of the *Catalpa*

The *Catalpa* set sail from New Bedford on 29 April 1875. Breslin and Desmond arrived in plenty of time to make contact with the prisoners at Fremantle and, by the time the ship eventually arrived in Fremantle, the local plans were ready.

The crew of the *Catalpa* consisted of sailors from places like the Azores and the Malay peninsula. This was a typical crew of the time. The Clan had its man on board, one Denis Duggan. The journey went well and Captain Anthony was even catching quite a number of whales which would help with the expenditure of the trip. The ship arrived at length at the port of Bunbury, near Fremantle, on 26 March 1876, 11 months after leaving America. Again one can only imagine how such a long voyage would have affected those aboard. They would have encountered other ships and landed at various ports on the way there, but the majority of time would have been spent ploughing through the mighty oceans with its attendant vagaries of weather.

But they had arrived safely – now the question was – would they be returning with their extra six passengers?

Arrangements for the flight of the IRB men

John Breslin, immediately after his arrival in Fremantle, made contact with the prisoners through a former convict who had recently been released. By a stroke of good luck too, he was invited into the prison only to be really alarmed at the tight security inside. He was also getting a little anxious about the delay in the arrival of the *Catalpa* and he knew, through his contact with James Wilson, one of the IRB men, that the rest of the men were also getting a bit uneasy. But at least further tangible help had come when a man called King, who was a member of the Australian IRB, arrived in the town with money for the escape plans. He also agreed to remain to assist with the escape itself, which pleased Breslin and Desmond.

No sooner had Breslin and King made all the arrangements they could for the time being when another mystery emerged. They discovered two rather shady looking characters moving about the town and the prison. King decided to approach them as he was convinced that they were spies but, when he did speak to them, he was happy that they were genuine. Believe it or not, these two men, Walsh and McCarthy, were Irish and they too had come to help the IRB prisoners. It seems almost incredible that, in this far corner of the world, there should now be three different groups of men, American, Australian and Irish, there on the same mission to assist in the rescue. They wisely, and quickly, coordinated their separate plans and worked closely together in the time remaining before the eventual arrival of the *Catalpa*.

At last the ship arrived and docked at Bunbury and Breslin immediately set out to interview Captain Anthony in order to finalise their plans for the rescue. It was agreed that the six men should be rescued from Rockingham beach about 20 miles south of Fremantle. A rowboat from the *Catalpa* would be there to take them out to the ship which would be fairly far out, maybe ten or twelve miles distant. They fixed the date for 6 April only to discover, to their dismay, that the Royal Navy ship *HMS Conflict* was visiting Fremantle and, as it would have been a much faster ship than *Catalpa*, they decided to wait until it had gone. It left on 11 April and a new date was agreed for Easter Monday, 17 April. Everything was now prepared – all that was now needed was a certain amount of good fortune and no further changes of plan.

Captain Anthony himself, together with some of his trusty crew, manned the rowboat and set out for Rockingham beach. They were experienced rowers and did not want to jeopardise the mission by having untried men on the oars. It was a sensible decision and they landed at the rendezvous point in good time. Meanwhile in Fremantle, Breslin and Desmond had two carriages and once the prisoners had escaped – without any difficulty as it happens – they sped off towards Rockingham. They arrived without a hitch and got the six men settled into the rowboat ready for their crossing to the *Catalpa*. All continued to go well until the crew spotted a number of people standing on the beach not far from their boat. This was unusual as the area was generally a very deserted place, especially at that early hour. They were even more alarmed to see one of the onlookers quickly mount a horse and ride off at speed towards Fremantle. They feared their plans had been foiled and so they started their sea crossing with a degree of urgency. Later on, as it transpired, police arrived at the beach only to discover, of course, that the rowboat was well out to sea.

After many hours of strenuous rowing, the sixteen men on board the rowboat espied the *Catalpa* and they were relieved that they would soon be on board. But yet more trouble loomed when another ship, the *Georgette*, was seen heading towards the escapees. The *Catalpa* was aware of what was happening and so it hurried towards the other ship which had on board a number of policemen. By the skin of their teeth, the *Catalpa* just managed to reach the rowboat before the *Georgette* and speedily took the exhausted men aboard. The rowboat had been at sea for 28 hours and it was a miracle that the rowers had been just about able to reach the *Catalpa* first. The *Georgette* left the scene to return to Fremantle and the men thought all would be well and that their journey home would now begin. But, once again, there were more potential stings in the tail. After refuelling, the *Georgette* was ordered to chase and board the *Catalpa*. It reached its quarry very quickly and demanded the return of the prisoners. Captain Anthony then truly proved his worth as the worthy leader of this audacious rescue. As his was an American ship, he hoisted the American flag and, although he clearly understood the order given by the captain of the *Georgette*, a British ship, he refused to accede to his demands and, giving no further quarter, sailed off, leaving the *Georgette* and its crew to lick their wounds. The men were on their way to freedom. The daring adventure had been a complete success.

The journey home and the aftermath

The long voyage home now began. News of the dramatic escape took some time to reach both America and England as the undersea cable had been deliberately severed thus causing major delays in transmitting messages. The Americans were delighted that the men were on their way home and that their exertions to fund the rescue had come to fruition in such a manner. The British, however, were less than pleased and the Prime Minister, Benjamin Disraeli, continued to oppose the release of IRB military prisoners. What he thought of the slick operation that had freed the prisoners is but one of conjecture. Perhaps, in private at any rate, he too may have considered the rescue as a clever and very effective operation. In Ireland, when the news was heard, there were countless parties and celebrations with the men's supporters cocking a snoop at the Castle administration.

However, to return to the journey home itself, all did not run smoothly. Relations between Duggan, the Clan's man on board, and Breslin became very unpleasant and Duggan suddenly tried to set the rescued men against Breslin and the captain. The situation further deteriorated when Captain Anthony wanted to start catching some whales to help with the expenses of the trip but the former prisoners demanded being taken home as quickly as possible. They even wrote a formal letter to Breslin with this demand and said they wanted to land at the nearest port in America without delay. And so the *Catalpa* headed straight for New York where it arrived on 19 August, four months after leaving Western Australia. There was no welcoming party because the original arrangements were that they should arrive at Fernandina in Florida. However John Devoy managed to get to New York fairly quickly and welcomed the six men home. He was, however, disturbed to hear about the altercations and disputes that had occurred on the way home. He was astonished to hear of the way that the prisoners had treated Breslin who had, after all, risked life and limb to effect their rescue. But the men were safely back and the rescue had been a complete success. When Captain Anthony returned to New Bedford he was given a hero's welcome and, although he received compensation for his trials and tribulations, he was no longer able to enter British ports whilst on his whaling expeditions.

The entire cost of the rescue of the six men was $26,000 and the man whose brainchild it had been, John Devoy, became nothing short of a legend amongst the Irish Americans right until his death in 1928.

This remarkable story is just part of the intricate web of events which can never fail to impress; never fail to astound and which never fail to encourage the inquisitive to find out more about Ireland's rich and amazing history.

Curious for more?

I can recommend these books for further reading:

McDonnell, Vincent, *The Catalpa Adventure – Escape to Freedom*, Cork, Collins Press, 2010.

O Luing, Sean, *Fremantle Mission*, Tralee, Anvil Books, 1965.

Stevens, Peter F., *The Voyage of the Catalpa – a Perilous Journey and Six Irish Rebels' Flight to Freedom*, New York, Carroll & Graf, 2002.

For books that aren't in common circulation I may be able to source them for you. Email me at clive.scoular@gmail.com or check out my website – *clivescoular.com*.

The Theft of the Irish Crown Jewels

Notice issued by the Dublin Metropolitan Police

HAVE YOU EVER had the pleasure of visiting the Tower of London to view the British Crown Jewels and, at the same time, wonder how on earth the Queen manages to balance that crown on her head during her delivery of the Queen's speech in the House of Lords chamber? If you have seen them, then I'm sure you were astounded at their beauty. I wonder then if you have ever seen the Scottish Crown Jewels which are kept at Edinburgh Castle. They certainly are very fine and would have adorned a number of monarchs' heads. And now I ask if you have ever seen the Welsh Crown Jewels? I hardly think so as Wales is a Principality and not a kingdom with the Prince of Wales as, shall we say, its principal personage.

Have ever heard of the Irish Crown Jewels and have you ever seen them? It's been a long time since there was a monarch in Ireland or even a chieftain which might be the more appropriate title. And how could they be Crown Jewels – after all there hasn't been a crowning of a monarch in Ireland in recent centuries. But there were special, and very expensive and beautiful, jewels which were commonly known as the Irish Crown Jewels. They did not consist of the usual crown and orb or sceptre, but simply a star and badge, each attached to delicate ceremonial ribbons. King William had presented them to the Most Illustrious Order of St Patrick, founded back in 1783, in 1831.

Mind you, these valuable pieces were composed of the most magnificent rubies, emeralds and Brazilian diamonds, all mounted in silver. They were extremely valuable and cost £65,000 which, for just two pieces of jewellery, was an enormous sum (perhaps several millions in today's prices).

And who were these Knights of St Patrick? They were a group of titled men who rose to prominence in Ireland and were chosen by the monarch or the Lord Lieutenant of Ireland to join this elite corps of noble gentlemen. There were never more than 24 of them at any one time which meant that there were not many occasions when a new knight was invested. Only when one of the Order died, was another chosen to succeed him.

Sir Arthur Vicars

The jewels were kept in the strong room at the Bedford Tower in Dublin Castle, the seat of British administration at that time. The person in charge of this regalia was Sir Arthur Vicars who had a rather unusual title – the Ulster King of Arms. He had held this post, which could hardly have been described as very onerous, for a number of years. He was very friendly with Frank Shackleton, brother of the Antarctic explorer, Sir Ernest Shackleton, and, as well as living in the same home apartments as Shackleton, had appointed him as Assistant Secretary in the Office of Arms. Vicars could best be described as a fussy little man who often took his visitors down to see the Crown Jewels by way of impressing upon them how important a custodian of regalia he was. Security tended to be rather lax mainly on account of the Dublin Metropolitan Police Headquarters being just across the castle yard in the neighbouring tower.

Around 1903 Vicars discovered that his post as Ulster King of Arms was entitled to attract a team of custodians to help him. And so he set about expanding his personal empire by making three further appointments. His friend Shackleton, who was reputedly a financial expert, also became the Dublin Herald; his nephew, Pierce Gun Mahony, (much to his father's displeasure – he being a Nationalist and his son a Unionist) Cork Herald; and an Englishman, Francis Bennett Goldney, the Athlone Pursuivant. The only time that these men would ever be needed in Dublin would be at the investiture of a Knight of St Patrick which, as we have seen, would be infrequently, although if they happened to be in Dublin, they would call in at their offices in the Bedford Tower. But Sir Arthur had conscientiously filled these 'necessary' posts, which further boosted his ego.

What was happening in Dublin at this time?

We all know how turbulent Ireland's history was around the turn of the twentieth century, what with a burgeoning interest in Ireland's art, culture and language and the talk of Home Rule. But, if the truth be told, the first decade was relatively quiet. There were many new plays written by Irish playwrights being performed at the Abbey Theatre, for example, and life was rather undisturbed. Arthur Griffith had founded Sinn Fein in 1905; Maud Gonne was orchestrating some anti Boer War demonstrations in the early years of the 1900s and, in the castle, the British administration under the dour Scots Lord Lieutenant, Lord Aberdeen, and the Chief Secretary, Augustine Birrell, was coasting along.

In the Bedford Tower

For some reason Vicars decided that they needed a new safe and an order was despatched. The only problem was that when the new safe arrived it would not fit into the strong room – it was too big to go through the door. Instead of ordering a more suitable one, and perhaps ticking off the feckless official who had requisitioned it, Vicars just set the new safe outside the door of the strong room. And there it stood, presumably causing an obstruction for everyone moving along the corridor where it was situated.

On 11 June 1907 Sir Arthur showed the jewels to an English visitor – and this was the last time they were ever seen.

The discovery of the disappearance of the Crown Jewels

Sir Arthur had, in his employ, a cleaner called Mary Farrell. She was always the first person to arrive at the tower and her duties entailed keeping the offices, and particularly Sir Arthur's office, spick and span. As she arrived on 3 June she reached into her handbag to get the key to open the door of the tower. But she discovered the door unlatched and unlocked. Something was wrong so she reported the incident to her supervisor, William Stivey, when he arrived for work. He was a little concerned so he, in turn, informed Sir Arthur. But his reaction baffled Stivey – the Ulster King of Arms just shrugged his shoulders and told his messenger to get on with his daily tasks. Vicars appeared completely nonchalant and unconcerned.

It should be noted that a very important visitor was due to arrive in Dublin in a week's time to invest a new Knight of St Patrick, Lord Castletown. The King himself was to be present at the investiture and he was due to stay for a couple of days, during which time he would not only carry out these official duties but would also have time to spend at his beloved horse racing at the Fairyhouse races.

On 6 June, Mary Farrell made another disturbing discovery. This time she found the strong room door unlocked. Whilst the safe was not inside the room for the reasons already given, she still felt that Stivey should tell Sir Arthur as quickly as possible. He left his boss a note to tell him what Mary Farrell had found and again, upon his return, considered Vicars indifferent and unworried. And then Vicars did something even more unusual – he gave Stivey the key to the safe and asked him to lodge a ceremonial ribbon inside it. Stivey was apprehensive for he had never before been asked to do any such thing. In fact he was a little suspicious and wondered why Sir Arthur had sent him on this errand. Then he made a startling discovery. When he came to the safe it was open and the jewels therein had vanished. The Irish Crown Jewels had disappeared – they had been stolen. Other precious items were also missing, but nothing to compare with the theft of the valuable star and badge.

Panic sets in

Vicars took fright. Instead of calling in the detectives, he summoned the Chief of the Dublin Metropolitan Police, Sir John Ross. Then he proceeded to talk incoherently and to lie, shift the blame and do anything possible to divert attention from himself – the keeper of the Irish Crown Jewels. He even denied that he had been told the strong room door was open – a message that had been brought to him a few minutes earlier by a stunned William Stivey. Investigations commenced which, after a full day of interviews, left Sir Arthur definitely not covering himself with glory. How many keys were there to the safe? Vicars replied that there were just two and he held both of them. One was always on his person on a key ring at his waist and the other was secreted away in a drawer in his apartment. Things were not looking good. When asked if there was any other information that should be mentioned, Sir Arthur replied in the negative and did not even mention the incidents involving the unlatched and open doors reported by Mary Farrell earlier in the week. The finger of suspicion pointed, at this moment anyway, at the Ulster King of Arms himself.

The police interrogations continued on the arrival in Dublin of Vicars's three associates who had been urgently summoned to answer questions. Young Mahony came quickly from his home in the south of Ireland and eventually Goldney and Shackleton, who had been in Italy, entered upon the scene. From these latter two men there emerged a couple of doubtful stories which revolved around the fact that neither of them thought that the jewels were carefully enough looked after. Shackleton often gossiped that the jewels were very likely to be stolen some day given the rather sloppy way Sir Arthur looked after them. The Dublin police realised that this whole affair was a pretty kettle of fish.

A lock expert was then brought in to give his opinion as to how the safe might have been opened. The safe had not been blown, picked or damaged in any way – it had been a simple matter of using a key or an exact facsimile to open it. Things were not looking good for Sir Arthur although he continued to deny any involvement.

To crown the embarrassment felt by the Office of the Herald, King Edward and Queen Alexandra arrived for their visit. On learning of the theft, the King was none too pleased – to put it mildly. He expressed his indignation and displeasure to Lord Aberdeen and quickly realised that he would not be investing Lord Castletown as he had expected although he could, at least, visit the Fairyhouse races. So the King had come to Dublin and returned to London without fulfilling his scheduled engagement and insisted that Vicars should be sacked from his job.

Soon there was another visitor. Inspector John Kane from Scotland Yard had been summoned to assist in the job of finding the jewels much to the chagrin of the men of the local police.

And then the mystery deepened.

Where are the jewels?
Early on in the investigation it was discovered that the star and badge had been delicately and painstakingly detached from the ribbons to which they had been attached. The ribbons had been left in the safe but the jewels had vanished. Who on earth would have taken the time to sit down on a chair after taking the jewels from the safe and unpick them with consummate care? Rather than just grabbing the regalia after opening the safe, the thief had taken time to carefully detach the ribbons. This would have taken some considerable time which immediately gave credence to the possibility, or the probability, of this being an 'an inside job'.

Then the most extraordinary decision was made. A clairvoyant should be brought in to assist in the discovery of the jewels. And so a lady with these specific skills was led into the interview room at the castle and asked to, well do what clairvoyants do, use her very specific skills to find the missing star and badge. She took her time whilst the puzzled investigators waited – and waited – and waited. At length she indicated that they would be found in a field down in the midlands of Ireland. Without hesitation, the police hurried off to the appointed place only to discover – or rather, not to discover – the hiding place of the jewels. Their searches had drawn a complete blank.

What next?

Fingers of suspicion started to be pointed – at Vicars and Shackleton principally. Vicars accused his erstwhile friend and financial advisor, Frank Shackleton, of knowing the whereabouts of the regalia. In turn Shackleton censured Vicars for being so careless in their custody. Vicars also knew that Shackleton had a rather shady crony, a former soldier called Richard Gorges, whom he considered a likely candidate as the jewel thief. The King, back in London, was becoming increasingly impatient. He demanded action and constantly harassed the hapless Aberdeen for a resolution to this embarrassing predicament. There were even regular debates in the House of Commons about the case. Everyone was demanding answers but none were to be found.

The King, totally dissatisfied with the situation and seeing the problem still unresolved after three months, bade – yea ordered - Lord Aberdeen to sack Sir Arthur from his post. And so Vicars was relieved of the post which he had held for many years. But he was determined not to take his dismissal without a fight. He would show what he was made of and enter into a struggle for his rights. He declared that he had not stolen the jewels so why was he being dismissed. In truth no one expected this turn of events, neither the King nor the Lord Lieutenant. Vicars, it seemed, was made of sterner stuff. At the same time Goldney and Shackleton were dismissed from their honorary roles. Strangely however, Gun Mahony was neither asked nor compelled to resign, although he did voluntarily leave his post to take up the law in 1910.

Vicars then prepared himself for the fight to save his name – and his job. He needed a barrister with a sound reputation and he chose young Gun Mahony's father, The O'Mahony, to defend him. This was a clever choice. Vicars was a Unionist and a great supporter of the establishment; O'Mahony, it will be remembered, was a Nationalist and one of those very keen to see the British removed from Ireland. This combination would surely work well. They set about preparing Vicars's defence before what they hoped would be a Royal Commission. But the King would not countenance this and refused his consent to it. However Lord Aberdeen agreed to what was called a Vice Regal Commission which would fit the bill.

After many months had passed and still without any resolution in sight, the three-man commission, consisting of a judge and two other learned gentlemen, met in a room in the very scene of the crime in the Bedford Tower. Vicars and O'Mahony turned up together with many others whose evidence would be vital. But, after just ten minutes, they had left the room when they discovered, for the first time, that witnesses would not be required to give evidence under oath. This then being the case, they decided against presenting their side of the affair. But the commission simply continued with the case allowing everyone else to submit their evidence without the legal intervention from Vicars's team. Shackleton, Goldney and young Gun Mahony, along with many others, had their evidence scrutinised by the commissioners and their lawyers. After a week, no blame had been attached to anyone apart from Sir Arthur himself. Shackleton and Goldney, the chief dramatis personae, were exonerated. Shackleton was clearly a suspect but, after a shaky start, he was able to bamboozle the commissioners declaring that 'anyone could have borrowed Vicars's keys to get into the safe'. When the hearing was finally concluded, Sir Arthur was publicly pilloried and charged with not having exercised due vigilance and proper care as custodian of the regalia. It was all over and he had not even been there to defend himself. It was his own fault, and in some ways it was – it might have been more advantageous for him to remain present and hear what the witnesses had to say even if he was not entirely approving of the circumstances. Be that as it may, he was sent packing once and for all to deepest county Kerry, never to return to his office and private empire in the Bedford Tower.

There is always an aftermath – a raking over of the coals

The press, both in Dublin and in the rest of the British Isles, was full of the story and, needless to say, Sir Arthur Vicars did not come out of it well. He had been charged and found guilty of a dereliction of duty; he had been unceremoniously sacked and banished from his office; a successor as Ulster King of Arms, Neville Wilkinson, had been appointed and his bête noir and erstwhile financial advisor and best friend, Frank Shackleton, had been let off Scot-free. There was little else to do but take the train south to spend his remaining days fuming over his fate. He was not a happy man.

But Vicars had a sting in the tail with which to vex the Castle administration. As he was leaving his office he was asked to hand over all his official keys. He refused, kept the keys in his pocket and headed off before anyone could do anything about it. This meant, of course, that the strong room and the safe could not now be opened, together with the many other places which needed a key. How embarrassing was this for the officials? Very embarrassing was the answer. Just a day or two after the departure of the disgraced Ulster King of Arms, some of the remaining regalia, and particularly the Sword of State, were required for a ceremony at the Castle. The sword was kept in the strong room, but the door was locked and the key in county Kerry. To resolve the matter, a young boy had to be brought up to the strong room and a number of workmen had to smash a hole in the wall big enough for the boy to be squeezed through to bring out the regalia. Strange and humiliating, but true. In modern day parlance, Sir Arthur had had the last laugh.

But the jewels were still missing. The papers constantly carried stories that someone knew where they were, only for it to be revealed as yet another wild goose chase. There continued to be regular debates in the House of Commons which epitomised the importance of the theft and the loss of such precious jewels. After a while the MPs from all other parts of the Kingdom were fed up with having to listen to, and spend valuable parliamentary time on, debates concerning this local Irish issue. The King kept enquiring of the Lord Lieutenant if they had been recovered and, to add spice to the story, the aforementioned 'financial advisor', Frank Shackleton, had been convicted of fraud and sent to jail. One can only imagine how Sir Arthur chuckled over these reports and newspaper articles. But still we must never exclude the possibility that he might have been the thief himself.

The ensuing years and the fortunes and misfortunes affecting those involved

Like all such tales of suspense and mystery, you will want to know what became of all these remarkable people, all of whom could well have been the culprit and thief of the Irish Crown Jewels. Let us therefore examine their fates.

Pierce Gun Mahony, as we will recall, was the only one of Sir Arthur's deputies to keep his job as Cork Herald. However he soon resigned of his own volition and was called to the Bar. But, in 1914, he met with a very violent death. At his home in county Kerry he had gone off to fish on a nearby lake one morning and, when he failed to return for his evening meal, a friend went down to the lakeside only to discover young Gun shot dead. No one ever resolved this mystery either – had he been shot or had he committed suicide?

Richard Gorges, that soldier bosom buddy of Shackleton, had been discharged from the Army and had taken to drink. He lived in Hampstead where he shot a policeman dead. He was indeed fortunate not to have been hanged for this heinous crime and it was while he was spending his long sentence in prison that, presumably being short of conversation with his cellmate, he mentioned that he had been involved in the theft of the Irish Crown Jewels. His companion, probably having no idea what Gorges was talking about, repeated the story to his guards in the prison. They would have told their superiors who, one has to surmise, considered the matter just another story of bravado and derring-do coming out of the mouth of an old lag. Gorges was eventually released from jail and lived a long life although he never seemingly regaled anyone else with this story. It would all have seemed far too unlikely and unbelievable – but one still wonders if there was any truth in it.

Frank Shackleton continued in his nefarious lifestyle. He defrauded a number of his wealthy and titled friends and a rumour went around that he was funding his brother, Ernest's, Antarctic expeditions from the money he had made from the sale of the Crown Jewels. This was soon discounted but did leave a sour taste in the mouths of those many respectable people who were working hard to make sure Ernest would reach the South Pole ahead of any of his rivals – which, of course, was sadly not to be the case. In 1912 a further warrant was issued for Shackleton's arrest. But there was a problem. He was in darkest Africa, Angola to be exact. He was pursued there by a determined detective who found him, arrested him and brought him back to the jurisdiction in England. There he was convicted and jailed once more. After his release, Ernest and his family, although very well aware of Frank's criminal past, stuck by him although they insisted that he change his name. So, for the rest of his life until his death in 1941, he was no longer Frank Shackleton of Irish Crown Jewels intrigue and infamy, but Frank Mellor.

Sir Arthur Vicars remained bitter and resentful. He firmly and regularly denied that he had stolen the jewels. He was living in a family house at Kilmorna, near Listowel in county Kerry. Over the ensuing years he continued to fight to prove his innocence and even won a libel case in 1913. But although he was a very unhappy man and having been thus far a bachelor, he did marry a sister of Pierce Gun Mahony's in 1917. In 1920, during the Irish War of Independence or the Black and Tan War, the IRA raided his home. They demanded, by a kind of twist of fate, the keys to his house safe which he refused to hand over. The raiders left empty-handed but returned the following year – on 14 April 1921 – to exact revenge. They set fire to his house (a regular fate for owners of Ireland's Big Houses in those troubled years) and, as Sir Arthur was trying to salvage some of his precious possessions, his attackers shot him dead. Thus ended the life of that one time Ulster King of Arms at the hands of those who would probably never have heard of such a man – he had simply been yet another of the Anglo-Irish gentry who were seen by the IRA as the epitome of those who had for centuries kept Ireland under unfair and unreasonable subjection.

Then who did steal the Irish Crown Jewels?

You decide. Perhaps it was King Edward VII who could conceivably have 'arranged' for the jewels to be taken since he certainly did not want any new Irish Nationalist government, if such ever came, to hold on to this valuable and distinctly British regalia. He might have thought that, if complete independence came after all the talk of Home Rule for Ireland, the Irish would take delight in perhaps selling the jewels which would have brought in 'a pretty penny'. The King would hardly have come disguised to Dublin himself to effect the theft but would have instructed one of his secret service people to purloin the jewels and return them to London.

Or maybe it was the Irish Nationalists who could have stolen the jewels knowing that it would be quite a coup to keep, after their hoped-for separation from England, part of the precious heritage of their soon-to-be former oppressors and perhaps realise their value to help fund their new state. There is another possibility however. The founder of Sinn Fein, Arthur Griffith, believed in a dual monarchy which meant that, even with Ireland free from the rest of the United Kingdom, they could still have a monarch of their own and so the regalia could become part and parcel of the ceremonies surrounding the crowning of a future king or queen in Dublin. This is not as preposterous as it seems although Griffith might have had some difficulty in persuading his colleagues to make the arrangements for such a coronation.

Then the Irish Unionists might have decided to arrange for the theft for they certainly did not want the Nationalists to get their hands on them. And they would be pleasing the King as well, for Unionists, after all, as loyal subjects, would see themselves doing the right thing.

Or had it been a professional thief who could have carried out the job although one cannot honestly imagine such a person sitting down on a chair with the star and badge in one hand and a needle in the other to unpick the ribbon from the regalia.

Was Francis Goldney a possible thief? Those who were well acquainted with him knew him to be a kleptomaniac although the chances of his involvement in this job do seem unlikely. However, after his death, a number of precious artefacts from Canterbury Cathedral were discovered in his home – so the question remains – was Goldney the one?

Surely then Frank Shackleton would be a distinct possibility for he knew where Vicars kept his keys and he himself was accustomed to being in and around the tower and its rooms, as well as being a regular visitor at Vicars's home. But why, if it was Shackleton, did he take the time to unpick the ribbons?

And how about Richard Gorges who could certainly have been the culprit for he knew Shackleton and could have 'borrowed' the keys? Perhaps both he and Shackleton could have worked together.

And how about Mary Farrell who does seem, on the face of it, a very unlikely thief? But she was always at the tower long before anyone else and would have been the most likely person skilled at unpicking ribbons. She could have had a son or a husband who might have had a shady background and they could have bribed her to get the jewels to them and then proceed to get rid of them.

And the final possibility could have been William Stivey who spent lots of time in the tower and knew where everything was kept. He could have taken Vicars's keys and effected the theft and, like Mary Farrell, could have had some shifty friends.

The jewels were never found
The story of the theft of the Irish Crown Jewels has now been told, or at least the most intriguing parts. These two items, the star and badge, were phenomenally valuable and if they were taken by a 'fence' and passed on to some disreputable 'receiver', they would

need to have been broken up and sold in small pieces. One thinks of Amsterdam as a likely place to find people skilled in the trade of passing on stolen jewels but, after all these years, it seems very unlikely that even a small piece of the Irish jewels could be found and, what's more, identified as part of the star and badge. It is now up to you to try to solve this conundrum and to forward to this author a small percentage of the takings by contacting him at his email address. This would only seem fair to recompense the one who had brought this mystery to your attention.

By the way I myself think that Frank Shackleton is the likely culprit but if you prove otherwise, and give your reasons, I'd be pleased to hear from you.

Curious for more?

I can recommend these books for further reading:

Bamford, Francis and Bankes, Viola, *Vicious Circle – the Case of the Missing Irish Crown Jewels*, London, Max Parrish, 1965.

Cafferky, John and Hannafin, Kevin, *Scandal and Betrayal – Shackleton and the Irish Crown Jewels*, Cork, Collins Press, 2002.

Dungan, Myles, *The Stealing of the Irish Crown Jewels – an Unsolved Crime*, Dublin, TownHouse, 2003.

For books that aren't in common circulation I may be able to source them for you. Email me at clive.scoular@gmail.com or check out my website – *clivescoular.com*.

William Butler Yeats

William Butler Yeats, painted by his father

WILLIE WAS BORN in Dublin on 13 June 1865 and was the eldest of the six children of John Butler and Susan Yeats. His father was at that time a lawyer and it seemed that he would progress well in this fairly lucrative profession – but this, however, was not to be. His mother was a Pollexfen, whose family owned a shipping business based in Sligo. To all intents and purposes there ought not to have ever been any financial strains on a family with such a pedigree. His parents even owned two properties in Celbridge and in Dublin which ought to have been another source of steady income for the family – this was not to be either.

As the family grew with Willie being followed by two brothers, Jack and Bobby, and three sisters, Lily, Lolly and Jane, their family circumstances changed. Sadly both Bobby and Jane, aged just three years and ten months respectively, died leaving John and Susan with their four remaining children to bring up and educate.

John Yeats decided that the law was not for him and that he would pursue his love of painting. They moved to London in the late 1860s and, for the succeeding ten years, moved house on eight occasions. This itinerant lifestyle did not suit Susan, and the children suffered accordingly. However it should be said at the outset that John B. Yeats turned out to be a most accomplished artist and he attracted many worthwhile commissions. But John B. had a problem – he rarely finished a portrait and, therefore, was rarely paid for his work thus leaving a lot of well-heeled patrons with a sour taste in their mouths. John's name was mud and the family continued to suffer; they lived in near poverty for years and, had it not been for financial aid rather reluctantly given by the Pollexfens, the Yeatses would have been in the poorhouse.

Young Willie had a shaky educational start in life. He learned what he could from his parents and his grandparents when he was in Sligo. He loved going over to Ireland for his holidays and for nearly two and a half years from 1872, the family stayed in Sligo. Willie loved the surroundings, the open air and the chance to mix with the local people. He found his grandparents, to use his own words, rather scary but he realised life was infinitely better in Sligo than in near abject poverty in London.

Willie then returned to London to live with his father while the rest of the family remained in Sligo. It was another testing experience for the young boy. His father, poor as he was at completing his commissions, was nonetheless gaining a respectable reputation. Perhaps life would improve and financial burdens would disappear. But again this was not to be – John decided to give up portrait painting and take up landscape painting. Life took yet another nosedive and making ends meet was almost impossible for the lad and his father. But even in the midst of this time of struggle, Willie and his father did forge a close familial tie and a mutual respect one for another. Willie was sent to Godolphin school where he did make progress, but he had to face difficulties from his fellow pupils who thought him rather odd, to say the least. But Willie was proud to announce, when quizzed about his father's occupation, that his Dad was an artist. These rather uncomfortable days and trying life circumstances were to make WB Yeats, the name we know and respect to this day, into the poet and playwright of world renown.

He left school at sixteen. His teachers considered Willie a good lad and certainly an interesting one for they freely admitted that very few of their pupils ever spouted poetry at them as Willie often did. And he was the kind of boy who was keen to enter into debates about world matters rather than simply talking about what teenage boys would normally do. He had left his mark at school and a very positive one at that.

Willie did not apply to enter Trinity College in Dublin and his father, though disappointed since he himself had been there, decided to send Willie to the Dublin Metropolitan School of Art. In many ways he thought that, if academic life was not destined for his eldest child, then maybe an artistic life would be a worthy alternative. But this didn't work out either. Willie wouldn't be a painter but what profession would he follow?

Poetry, mysticism – and Nationalism

A change was taking place in Willie's life. He met the county Armagh poet George Russell (AE) who was to exert a huge influence on him. He was soon attracted to mysticism which greatly disturbed his father; he was soon trying to understand the changes taking place in Irish society; he was quickly beginning to appreciate the impact that CS Parnell and Michael Davitt had had on Ireland.

But even more importantly Willie had blossomed as a poet and his life and career were soon to be devoted to the arts. By the age of 20 he had published his first book of poems. Poetry had become his reason for living. He joined clubs where he could immerse himself in the works of other luminaries in the field of the arts. He got to know people like Douglas Hyde and it was not long before he fell under the spell of the old Fenian, John O'Leary. He now started to understand republicanism and the Catholic dimension. The safety net of his Anglo-Irish upbringing was soon to be exposed to the realities of life in Ireland. The people he met and mixed with knew they were in the presence of, if not exactly greatness, then certainly a poetic and artistic genius. And he was just this young man whose path in life had only now been drawn out.

Life moved quickly. He became a close friend of the poetess, Katharine Tynan, who thought that Willie's poetry was awe-inspiring. He even proposed marriage to Katharine who, thankfully for such an inexperienced young man, turned him down.

He was settling well in Dublin, getting to know the great and the good when it was again decided that the family should return to London. He was reluctant to move but there was no alternative. But they did at least move to a much better house in the model Bedford Park estate and the Yeatses actually began to flourish. Before long Willie was meeting many celebrated and famous people such as Oscar Wilde and Rudyard Kipling. He was making some money by contributing his poems to local journals and, although still not wholly independent from his family, he knew he had chosen the right profession.

It was around this time too that he encountered Maud Gonne and he very quickly fell in love with her. She nearly drove him crazy of course with her rigid views on life. He was developing an interest in the occult and it took some years to get these ideas out of his mind. But life changed again for Willie when he met Lady Augusta Gregory.

The Irish theatre blossoms

Meeting Lady Gregory was probably the single most important event in his life. He was invited to her home at Coole Park in county Galway and, from the mid 1890s until his marriage in 1917, Willie Yeats spent almost every summer there. He was given the run of the house and the lovely grounds and he was able to compose and write to his heart's content. In truth she was his fairy godmother who treated him as her own son. When JM Synge, the playwright, became another regular visitor at Coole, the future of an Irish theatre was assured. They met, discussed, contemplated and turned their wonderful ideas into a glittering reality.

There were, however one or two blips during the 1890s. He repeatedly asked Maud Gonne to marry him, but she resolutely kept refusing him. It might be interesting for a future biographer to thoroughly diagnose the underlying reason for his persistent proposals over so many years. In due course, Willie even asked Maud's daughter Iseult (by her French lover, Lucien Millevoye), to be his wife – but she too turned him down. And, almost to add insult to injury, Willie was dumbfounded to discover that his beloved Maud had married John McBride in 1903. It took him a long time to get over this rebuff; in fact, he never actually did. And McBride was to die an Irish martyr after the Easter Rising in 1916.

Another sadness occurred in the very early days of the new millennium – Susan Yeats died leaving the family bereft and thinking of the tough and itinerant life their mother had endured. John clearly missed his wife yet he, as we will see, was to make a life changing decision himself when he left to live in the United States.

By 1904, the Abbey theatre opened its doors much to everyone's delight. Willie's play 'The Countess Cathleen' had been performed in Dublin five years earlier in 1899 and he was becoming a most prolific and popular playwright. His determination, and that too of Lady Gregory and John Synge, had come to fruition and many of their plays were now being regularly presented. And what was more, and particularly pleasing to the three directors, was that they now had Irish actors and actresses making up the cast of their plays. It may seem obvious to us today to have local actors speaking the parts in Irish plays but it must be remembered that, in the early days, Irish works had to be performed by actors from Britain who did not have the correct accents and did not fully appreciate the meaning of the words they were speaking. The Abbey had transformed the Irish stage, thanks to the hard work, wisdom and tenacity of Gregory, Synge and Yeats.

The thriving Yeats family

It was not only Willie who was keeping the Yeats family name to the fore in Dublin and London society. Willie had been writing play after play which were proving to be big hits, not only in Britain and Ireland, but also in the United States. He travelled to America in 1903, the year before the Abbey opened its doors. The visit was a hearty success with his plays attracting full houses wherever he went.

Back at home his two sisters, Lily and Lolly, were also making names for themselves. They set up companies which produced embroidery and linen goods and then opened what was to become their greatest enterprise, the Cuala Press, which published books for many local and thriving authors. This press was to continue from these early days of the 20th century until well after the Second World War.

Willie's brother, Jack, as well as his father, were artists of renown and, whilst they continued sometimes to let their customers down when they failed to finish commissions, nonetheless they were amongst the finest painters in the land. The indomitable Sarah Purser came to the aid of father John when she set up, at her own expense, an exhibition of his works and those of another unsung painter, Nathaniel Hone. This was Sarah's way of saying – 'come and support these brilliant Irish painters, they are the best in the land'. And it worked because, from then on, both artists were to prove even more popular. Sarah Purser was always an indefatigable supporter of the Irish arts and, as we would say today, she was always prepared to put her money where her mouth was.

Difficult years at the Abbey – challenging years for Ireland
When JM Synge's play 'The Playboy of the Western World' opened on the Abbey stage turmoil rather than calm ensued. Was not JM Synge the finest of Ireland's playwrights? Those who bayed for Synge's blood at those early performances clearly did not understand, or did not want to understand, the reality of Irish life. Synge's plays were powerful and spoke of life as it really was. For too long theatre

audiences had been used to seeing plays which, to put it bluntly, had a happy ending regardless of the trials and tribulations of the story being performed. Yeats was present when these outbursts occurred and, without even a second thought, strode on to the stage, mid performance, and berated and condemned the protesters. He told them that their attitude to such an excellent play showed them up in a light of pure ignorance. His heated remarks did have some effect although riots on stage, not only in Dublin but also in America, were to feature for some years to come.

During the years of the Great War, two incidents of enormous significance occurred. In September 1915, the *Lusitania* was sunk within sight of the city of Cork with the loss of hundreds of lives. Aboard was Sir Hugh Lane, Ireland's greatest art lover, who had wanted his best paintings to be housed in Dublin for the local population to visit and admire. He had, however, forgotten to sign a codicil to his will so bequeathing the paintings and, as he drowned when the ship went down, so the problems over their future emerged. He was a nephew of Lady Gregory and friend of Willie's and, for the succeeding years, regular difficulties occurred and the saga over where the paintings should be housed continued and, even to this day, the matter has not yet been satisfactorily resolved.

The Easter Rising, of course, broke out in April 1916. Willie was in England at the time and it was said that he 'fretted' at not being consulted! Some of his best and most vivid poetry was written at this time including his most moving poem 'Easter 1916' which contained the immortal words 'a terrible beauty is born'. He was upset because some of those executed had been friends of his and he was determined that they should be remembered in his poetry. John McBride, whose marriage to Maud Gonne had so incensed Willie, had, as we have already noted, also faced the firing squad.

During this decade he had been writing his best poetry and his popularity was on a high. He had accepted a civil list pension of £150 per annum, which, although clearly well deserved, was frowned upon by his Nationalist friends, and it took a little time for this faux pas to be forgotten. His friend and fellow Abbey director, JM Synge, had died in 1909 thus leaving the theatre bereft of perhaps its most talented playwright. It was also in 1916 that Willie bought a tower at Ballylee not far from Coole Park and this became known as Thoor Ballylee. The purchase price was £35.

Willie Yeats is married – and life goes on

Many of his friends considered that Willie would never marry especially after all his rejected proposals to Maud Gonne. But on 20 October 1917, he married George Hyde-Lees, the daughter of an acquaintance. She was a young lady less than half his age but they were to enjoy a most happy marriage. Willie was keen to bring George to live at Thoor Ballylee but then he heard of the death, in the final throes of the war, of Robert Gregory, Lady Augusta's only son. He was saddened by Robert's passing and consoled his friend at Coole Park. In February 1919, his daughter, Anne, was born in Dublin where they were once more resident.

Soon George and Willie headed off for another tour of America, leaving Anne in the care of her two aunts, Lily and Lolly. During this successful trip, Willie had the chance to see his father who had, by now, been resident there for some time. It was to be the last time they were to meet for John B. died in 1922. During that same year their son, Michael, was born. In Dublin it was a difficult time and especially so for Willie who had accepted an appointment to be a senator in the new Irish Free State's upper house. Again this decision proved contentious with his Nationalist friends but he worked hard at his new position, speaking on a number of occasions on topics that would affect the ordinary people of the new jurisdiction. He did occasionally embarrass his Anglo-Irish senator friends with some of his speeches like, for example, his ill thought out speech on divorce. But they all eventually forgave him – this was simply the Willie Yeats they had all come to understand.

In the midst of the War of Independence, their home at Ballylee was blown up and their house in Dublin was fired upon on at least one occasion. Willie Yeats realised that his various unpopular stances would attract hostile attention but he wanted to do his duty in the senate which he did until 1928. On the plus side, however, he was pleased to encourage the promotion of some excellent plays by Sean O'Casey being performed on the stage of an ever revitalised Abbey theatre, although there were more riots when 'The Plough and the Stars' was staged. Once again Willie came out from behind the stage curtain to berate the rowdy and unappreciative section of the audience.

In 1923 he was awarded the Nobel Prize and travelled to Stockholm to receive the accolade from the Swedish king. From the money he accepted as his prize, he and his family spent an extended holiday in Sicily and Italy, a country that he came to love.

The latter years of this artistic genius

By the end of the 1920s, Willie's health gave rise for concern. On holiday in Spain late in 1927 he suffered an attack of bleeding of the lungs although he soon recovered. He was still writing prolifically and his works were universally acclaimed. The family tended to spend more and more time away from Ireland, renting a flat in Rapallo, but they did continue to visit Dublin, Ballylee and Coole from time to time. The children attended boarding school in Switzerland although young Michael did attend St Columba's School in Dublin for a time where one of his best friends was Brian Faulkner, later in life to become Prime Minister of Northern Ireland.

He was ill again in 1929 and it was decided to give up the tower at Ballylee. When he was in Dublin he was busy setting up an Irish Academy of Letters and it was during this time that Lady Gregory died. Willie was devastated for, without doubt, it was she who had been responsible for his career. In truth it should also be said that perhaps Willie Yeats could have given more recognition to Augusta's contribution to his life for she had, after all, given him refuge and inspiration in his early and formative years as a poet and playwright.

He continued to visit America where his plays were ever more popular and he did, at last, have plenty of money to spend on his family and himself.

He attained his 70th birthday in 1935 and this birthday was acclaimed by hundreds of his friends and artistic acquaintances. But even as his health was deteriorating, he still kept writing with increased vim and vigour. His friendship with Sean O'Casey had hit the rocks in past years but he was reconciled with him as his play 'The Silver Tassie', over which there had been bad blood, was at last revived at the Abbey, despite clerical protests. He enjoyed broadcasting on BBC radio and still was not averse to lecturing and reprimanding unruly audiences. He seemed to come into his own in situations like these. He even had the pleasure of meeting with Maud Gonne again in these latter years which doubtless brought back memories.

Willie Yeats died on 28 January 1939 at Cap Martin in the south of France. His passing was mourned by many in the art world and particularly by members of his family. In 1948 his body was disinterred and he was reburied, controversially many would say as there has always been doubt as to whether or not it really was his body brought back from France, at Drumcliffe churchyard in county Sligo where thousands flock year in and year out to this day to gaze upon his simple gravestone inscribed with the words 'cast a cold eye on life, on death, horseman, pass by'.

Curious for more?

I can recommend these books for further reading:

Foster, R. F., *W. B. Yeats – a Life – 1. The Apprentice Mage*, New York, Oxford University Press, 1997.

Foster, R. F., *W. B. Yeats – a Life – 2. The Arch-Poet*, New York, Oxford University Press, 2003.

Hardwick, Joan, *The Yeats Sisters – a Biography of Susan and Elizabeth Yeats*, London, Pandora, 1996.

Mac Liammoir, Michael and Boland, Eavan, *W. B. Yeats*, London, Thames and Hudson, 1971.

Martin, Augustine, *W. B. Yeats*, Dublin, Gill and Macmillan, 1983.

For books that aren't in common circulation I may be able to source them for you. Email me at clive.scoular@gmail.com or check out my website – *clivescoular.com*.

Sean O'Casey

Sean O'Casey c.1920

JOHN CASEY, FOR that was his birth name, was born on 30 March 1880 and was the fifth, and last, child of Michael and Susan. They were active members of the Church of Ireland and lived, not as many people have said in the slums of Dublin, but in what might be described as an inner city parish. Like so many families in those years, not all of their children survived and this meant that, by the time John came along, he was many years younger than his older siblings. This did have an effect on his formative years although it has to be said that he had a very positive relationship with his parents. His father was a man of many parts, learned and well thought of in the community. He had a wonderful library at home and John delighted in reading many of these books – he became enthralled with Shakespeare in his early years, for example.

The older Casey children had a sound education in a fee paying school but, when their father died in 1886, when John was just six years old, the family's fortunes went dramatically into decline. During the subsequent years Susan had to juggle with what money she had which meant, amongst other difficulties, that the family had to, as we say nowadays, downsize and move to smaller and smaller houses. At the time they were living in a fairly substantial house in Upper Dorset Street, but then they needed to move down the property ladder to Inisfallen Parade. It also meant that with finances ever tighter, education for John suffered.

Early years

For John these early years were lonely. He did have a close relationship with his mother but his health was never robust. And to add to this he had a problem with his eyesight which was to affect him throughout his long life. He attended the local National School where, believe it or not, his own sister was the principal. Although there presumably could be no favouritism, nonetheless John was well looked after and given every encouragement to learn. He did well in his class tests and had a remarkable ability to memorise everything he learned.

As his two oldest brothers, Mick and Tom, left home to join the army and went off to get married, unions which found no favour with their mother, life became yet more difficult and intolerable as far as finances were concerned. This led to a further move to an even smaller home in Hawthorn Terrace.

When he was just nine John was taken away from school by his mother following an altercation which would have resulted in a public caning in front of his entire school. Susan was going to have nothing to do with this and so removed him. From then on his sister schooled him at home. This was to lead to difficulties in later life in making friends.

But life was not all doom and gloom

John proved to be a willing student at home and benefitted from his sister's diligent attention to the scholarly needs of her little brother. He continued to read the classics and enjoyed the writings of many well-known playwrights. In his early teenage years, his brother Isaac, who was seven years his senior, became interested in and enthused about amateur dramatics. He was ever on the hunt for small, disused halls in the area in which to stage plays. In this endeavour, and with John's help, many such venues became the scene of many productions which were not only enjoyed by the locals but, more importantly, gave budding actors and actresses their first chance to tread the boards. John himself performed in many of these plays and soon went on to participate in shows in the Mechanic's Institute, which was later to become the Abbey Theatre. He loved not only being an actor himself but also becoming a regular patron at every stage performance in the city of Dublin – well at least as many as he could afford to attend.

Another keen interest of John's was his parish church, St Barnabas, situated on the north side of the Liffey. He attended regularly and taught for some years in the Sunday school there. He was a faithful supporter of his rector who had problems, from time to time, with some rather bigoted Orangemen in his congregation. John stood up to these men and proved to be a really good friend to his pastor.

By the age of fourteen John got his first job as a despatch clerk at the princely weekly salary of 6/- (30p). After giving his mother her contribution, he diligently searched the city bookshops and bought copies of the works of the classical masters like Charles Dickens and Victor Hugo. But he soon lost this job and found it hard to find regular employment. He then became a navvy on the railway, a position hardly suited to this fragile young man. It goes without saying that this tough graft did not work out for John Casey. Another pattern of his life was shaping up – money, or rather the lack of it. And to add to the family's woes, another smaller house beckoned, this time in Abercorn Road although, by this time, there was only mother and John at home.

John becomes Sean and Casey becomes O Cathasaigh

By the early years of the 20th century life was radically changing for the young Casey. He had joined the Gaelic League with its love of the Irish language and all things Irish. This meant severing his Unionist links and, although old habits died hard, he did continue to attend church. He became the secretary of the Drumcondra branch of the League and started to become really involved with people of a Nationalist bent. He soon realised that membership of the League often drew men and women into the arms of the IRB, the Irish Republican Brotherhood. He decided quite quickly that he did not want to take this fundamental step so he never became associated with them. But he was a changed person and open to taking up what he saw as worthy causes against injustice and discrimination. By the age of 30 he had found a new champion, Jim Larkin.

Larkin, a Liverpudlian, had hit the Dublin scene with a vengeance. His sole aim in life was to ensure better conditions for the manual workers in the city. He set about insisting that every worker joined a union which was anathema to the employers in Dublin. A clash became inevitable with the workers becoming unionised and the employers forbidding their employees to join any union. In fact Sean lost his job because he refused to sign a declaration, as demanded by the employers, to say that he would not join up.

He continued to stick by Larkin although, without paid employment, life was financially catastrophic at home. His health, too, was giving rise to concern when he suffered from a paralysis of his legs. This prevented him from finding another job and for some considerable time he was only ever sporadically in employment.
It mattered little to Sean – he had found a champion to follow. But there was a downside to this fatal attraction. His newly found political views found no favour with any of the Nationalist groupings he was assiduously courting and so he simply resigned from all of them – this behaviour becoming one of his life's unbending traits.

The Great Lock Out and the Irish Citizen Army
All this radical action by Larkin was bound to lead to one outcome – a strike and a fight to the death. The auguries for a peaceful solution looked dim. And so it was that during 1913, having given their workers a final ultimatum, the employers locked out over 20,000 men. This became a truly tough time for the men and their families. Although there were many who came to the aid of the strikers to help feed their families, the workers had little alternative in the end but to submit and return to work – and for a reduction, and not an increase, in their wages. Sean had done all he could to help but without any success. Soon afterwards, James Connolly, another fighter for the needs of the downtrodden, arrived in Dublin and set up what he called the Irish Citizen Army. These men and women performed their duty during the Lock Out by protecting the workers from attacks by the employers. They helped to keep the peace and largely succeeded. Sean soon became the secretary of the ICA. This also gave him his

first chance to write articles for the Nationalist newssheets which proliferated at this time, titles such as 'The Irish Worker'. But, like so much that would shape his future life in dealing with people, Sean decided that he couldn't get on with those at the paper and within the ICA, including engaging in a very public spat with Constance Markievicz, and he promptly resigned his post as secretary

Larkin, Connolly and the Easter Rising

When James Larkin finally decided to get out of Dublin and go to the United States, he left James Connolly in charge. Sean didn't get on with Connolly, which meant that he had become completely disassociated with the people whose politics had initially excited him. And, when the Easter Rising broke out in April 1916, he took no part in it, which proved embarrassing to those who knew him like Connolly who was soon to be executed as a result of the uprising.

Sadness – and the first spark of genius

Sean's mother, Susan, died in 1919 and, by this time too his sister Bella and his brother Tom were also dead. It was a difficult time for Sean emotionally and financially and he even had trouble paying the funeral expenses. Soon after all these tragic events, his brother, Isaac, who had encouraged Sean in his younger days towards a career in the arts, decided to emigrate. In double quick time Sean found accommodation in Mountjoy Square. These were unhappy and sorrowful days for Sean but, even in the midst of these family heartbreaks, a couple of bright lights appeared at the end of the tunnel. He wrote his first story – 'The Sacrifice of Thomas Ashe' and then, in the troubled times with the Black and Tans roaming the streets of Dublin, the spark of one of his greatest plays – 'The Shadow of a Gunman' – emerged. And to add to his supreme efforts to overcome his melancholy, he met his first real love, a girl called Maura Keating. There was a part of Sean, who was by now almost 40 years old, that thought he would never fall in love or even marry but these ideas were dispelled with the chance of real companionship. He was visiting the Abbey Theatre again and felt driven to write more plays. Whether he realised it or not, Sean's theatrical genius was beginning to blossom and he was determined to write for the stage, and for the Abbey in particular. But his first three plays were rejected by Lady Augusta Gregory and WB Yeats. He was disappointed but he did take some encouragement from many positive points that Lady Gregory had made. By 1922 his 'Shadow of a Gunman' had finally been accepted. He would now have the pleasure of seeing his work performed on the stage of Dublin's premier theatre.

And he now changed his name again, he was no longer John Casey or Sean O Cathasaigh – he was Sean O'Casey. His star was rising in the firmament; his time had come; Sean O'Casey's name would soon be on everyone's lips.

A Playwright

There was good news and bad news as far as his first plays were concerned. The good news was that the Abbey Theatre was packed to the doors when his plays were being performed. The bad news was that, especially during the season when 'The Shadow of a Gunman' was on stage, these were tragic and heart-rending days for Ireland

– the Civil War was raging. At this distance in time it seems a wonder that such a play, based on this war, was so popular and that so many Dubliners were flocking to see it despite the dangers surrounding them. The theatre did have to close towards the end of the war and did not reopen until the late summer of 1923. Sean had a long wait for his first paltry payment of £4.

But the important thing for Sean was that he was now a playwright and recognised as such. Lady Gregory, true to form, was one of his greatest fans and supporters. Having discussed his previous rejected plays with him, Sean began to appreciate, and take note of, her wise advices and her enthusiasm for the impressive flow of language emanating from his works. He could now throw aside his navvy's shovel and thrust forth his chest – he was 'on his way'.

'Juno and the Paycock', yet another of O'Casey's plays known and enjoyed by all of us to this day, became another firm favourite; it was popular; it starred many of the theatre's up and coming actors and actresses and it played to full houses. The style and content of the play did, however, have its critics but its popularity usually overcame any opposition. However, this was not always to be the case.

Augusta Gregory, whose chief asset throughout her life was her knack of discovering dramatic and artistic geniuses, now became a close friend to Sean. To begin with he found the grand surroundings at Coole Park in county Galway a little daunting but he soon got to love the place and to get inspiration from it. But there was another side to Sean's personality – he tended to speak his mind before considering what he was about to say. He certainly was outspoken and his outbursts created tensions at the Abbey. The language in his plays, whilst incisive and insightful, was starting to cause offence, not only with the Abbey directors and actors, but also with his audiences. The truth was that what he was saying was essentially accurate and precise but it was probably too soon for theatre audiences to be quite ready for such realism. Deep down they clearly understood the meaning of what was being said; they just didn't want anyone to actually express it out loud.

His next play – 'The Plough and the Stars' – epitomised this. It opened in London and was well received, possibly because English audiences didn't fully appreciate the nuances of the words. It eventually opened in Dublin in the early part of 1926 to packed houses and much acclaim. But by the end of the first week on the Abbey stage, riots broke out in the theatre during the performance. It is hard to imagine the scene; who would ever consider getting up and throwing rotten tomatoes at the stage, say, in a theatre in Belfast? But this is exactly what happened – it seems probable that a group of determined opponents had come into the theatre with the sole intention of causing a riot. Sean was in the audience but secreted away in a corner somewhere. WB Yeats, as one of the Abbey's directors, came out on the stage and, having narrowly avoided various missiles heading for the actors on the stage, addressed the rioters and told them to come to their senses – in today's parlance, he gave them a piece of his mind. It did have some effect for the play was able to continue although with further frequent interruptions. The real reason for the ill will was the fact that 'The Plough' seriously debunked the Easter Rising which, so soon after the event, was touching too many raw nerves. It was time for Sean to go; he realised he had gone too far; he had to leave the city of his birth.

Self imposed exile – and marriage

His mind was made up, or it had been made up for him. He reluctantly decided that he would leave Dublin and left for England at the beginning of March 1926. He was now almost 46 years old and had become a playwright, and a talented one at that. He grieved that he could not continue to have his plays performed in Dublin but in many ways realised that he had brought this dire situation upon himself. What he excelled in the creation of great stage works, he seriously lacked in diplomacy and tact. He didn't want to stay in London but when he saw 'Juno' and 'The Plough' playing to packed houses in the West End, he had a change of mind. He had become an overnight sensation and an artistic celebrity and before long he was mixing with the great and the good in London. Lady Edith Londonderry and Sybil Thorndyke got to know him and they became firm friends. The famous artist, Augustus John, painted his portrait. This frail little man from the back streets of Dublin had achieved popularity, fame and, although not yet (or ever!) a fortune, and was now the toast of the town. He wasn't going to go back to Ireland now, although he did have qualms about his newfound fame.

His next play, 'The Silver Tassie', inspired by the Great War, was definitely his best play to date and it was accepted for the London stage. The Abbey directors, however, having deliberated for some considerable time, turned it down and it would be some time before an Irish audience was to see it in their own country. Mr O'Casey was now thinking that maybe London would be his domicile after all.

Sean continued to think that he would never marry – he was, after all, now in his mid forties. But all this was soon to change when he met a young Irish actress in London called Eileen Carey. Their love quickly blossomed and, with his plays continuing to find favour both in London and New York, the couple decided to marry. They tied the knot in the city of London on 23 September 1927 and soon found a little house in St John's Wood. On 30 April 1928 their son, Breon, was born.

He now decided to confront WB Yeats and Lady Gregory concerning their much-delayed decision not to stage 'The Silver Tassie' for he was more and more convinced that it was his best play to date. However, in modern day language, he rather shot his bolt in correspondence with the Abbey. He told Yeats exactly what he thought of him, although he did not want Lady Gregory to suffer from his invective as he realised that she was more in tune with his writing. He appreciated that it was probably more difficult for her to win her point when deciding what plays should be staged at the Abbey, especially because of the frequent unhelpful stances often taken by Yeats. The play did eventually open in London, but not until the end of 1929. It was an immediate and roaring success with all his new and titled English friends in attendance on the first night. Lady Gregory happened to be in London at this time and she appealed to Sean to let her come to see the performance and to meet with her. It was her way of trying to mend fences with O'Casey. But he refused her request and this rebuff turned out to be his greatest regret for the rest of his life. Lady Gregory died in 1932 and they never met again.

A chance to make some money

Despite his spats with the Abbey directors and their continued baulking of his plays, Sean now felt that, perhaps for the first time in his life, he would be more financially secure. After all, his plays were being performed in England and the United States to much acclaim. He and Eileen now looked forward to being able to bring some security to their lives. But this hope was quickly dashed with the Wall Street crash in 1929 which meant that his plays were taken off the stage both in America and sometimes even in London. This meant that they had to move out of London to Chalfont St James in Buckinghamshire – a move they were always to describe as the silliest one they had ever made. But Sean was still as prolific as ever and continued to write, although his style and content radically changed. Looking at Ireland from afar, he chose to expose what he saw as the merciless grip that both the Catholic Church and Eamon de Valera were exerting on the ever-dwindling population in the country of his birth. During the 1930s, those dreaded years of depression and the fear of an imminent worldwide conflict, he presented 'Within the Gates' and 'The Star Turns Red'. English audiences enjoyed these productions but they found no favour in Ireland where they were often censored. It seemed clear that Sean O'Casey, considered by the great and the good of the world's literati as one of the greatest Irish playwrights, would forever be persona non grata in Ireland.

It may have been a golden age for O'Casey's writing but it was quite the opposite when it came to paying the bills. Eileen had to return to the stage herself to help make ends meet and Sean's health worsened. His sight and the effects of his chain smoking meant that these years, which should have been happy, fulfilled and full of promise, were blighted by misfortune and disappointment.

Rather than enjoying a close relationship with the newspaper critics; rather than presenting himself as an enthusiastic and passionate writer of popular works for the stage; rather than showing himself as a happy contributor to the arts in an otherwise gloomy decade for the population, Sean O'Casey chose to carry on a barrage of criticism against many of these people who should have been his friends. New York, however, seemed to be enjoying his plays and he travelled there in September 1934 to supervise rehearsals for 'Within the Gates', a play which proved popular with his American audiences, despite some protests largely orchestrated by clergymen who managed to get the play banned for a short period. Nonetheless the play did run for over 100 nights, although he didn't make as much money as he had hoped from the performances over there. Poverty was destined to haunt him for the rest of his life.

The years approaching World War Two

In early 1935 the O'Caseys had their second child, a son called Niall. They were delighted and they hoped that life would change for the better. 'The Silver Tassie' finally opened at the Abbey in August with the usual divergence of opinions. The audiences, by now understanding Sean's dramatic skills, loved it; the Catholic clergy abhorred it and many of the newspaper critics lambasted it. But none of this was hardly a surprise to him – he just grinned and got on with life. In the same year Sean paid what was to be his last visit to Dublin where he was at last reconciled with WB Yeats.

In these years a number of his plays were being successfully made into films. 'The Plough' and 'Juno' became early box office hits on the silver screen and both Eileen and Sean felt that, at last, they would make some money. They were even invited to come to live in America but, having given the proposal some thought, they declined the offer and instead moved to Totnes in Devon.

There was more success for him when 'The Star Turns Red', after a shaky start, did well. By now war with Germany was looming and the London theatres started to close. Just as war was declared, their daughter, Shivaun, was born and at almost the very same time three London children were billeted on them. During the war, despite the responsibilities of bringing up a new baby and caring for the evacuee children, Sean continued to write and, in 1943, a performance of 'Red Roses for me' was premiered at the Olympia Theatre in Dublin. This play was regularly performed in England after the war and Sean and Eileen travelled to London to see it.

Sean O'Casey's twilight years

During the 1930s Sean had started to write his autobiography and, in the end, he wrote six volumes of memoirs. He continued to write more plays and started to point a finger at what he called 'Ireland's priest ridden society'. He saw Ireland's population, and especially its young people, emigrating and leaving the country with barely three million people. His plays highlighted this scandal as he saw it and, of course, he suffered the slings and arrows shot at him by the Catholic clergy and by de Valera and his weak willed colleagues.

His health continued to deteriorate and most especially his eyesight – it was not long until he was virtually blind. Yet he worked on relentlessly, producing play after play, answering his critics in the press and determined to keep going. His motto for life was that living was infinitely better than waiting to die.

The O'Caseys moved again in 1954 to the outskirts of Torquay and as usual Eileen had the problem of settling Sean into his new surroundings. But he did settle quickly and continued to write more, including 'The Bishop's Bonfire' which proved to be a terrific hit at the Gaiety Theatre and, as was the regular pattern, to incur the wrath of the church.

A tragedy struck the family in 1956 when their second son, Niall, contracted leukaemia and died aged just 21. They were utterly devastated but Sean would not let himself quit – he wrote and remembered his lovely son. This was Sean's way of getting over his son's death.

Sean was pleased to see that, by the late 1950s, Ireland was beginning to shake off its weary past and the theatres in Dublin were having more opportunities to savour the plays of Sean O'Casey. Many of these new plays, and his older ones as well, were being revived in the United States. He would have liked to have returned there, but he was too unwell. However Eileen went on more than one occasion and was able to report the enthusiastic headlines in the American papers. More films were being made which would keep the name of O'Casey to the fore.

His last play was entitled 'Behind the Green Curtains' and was full of fun, farce and laughter.

Sean O'Casey died, following a heart attack, on 18 September 1964 – he was 84 years old. The dramatic genius of this great Irishman had gone home but his work would survive him and bring pleasure and enjoyment to countless generations for the years to come.

Curious for more?

I can recommend these books for further reading:

Hunt, Hugh, *Sean O'Casey*, Dublin, Gill and Macmillan, 1980.

Murray, Christopher, *Sean O'Casey – Writer at Work*, Dublin, Gill and Macmillan, 2004.

For books that aren't in common circulation I may be able to source them for you. Email me at clive.scoular@gmail.com or check out my website – *clivescoular.com*.

John Millington Synge

A sketch of Synge c.1906

WHAT DO IRISHMEN and women know about JM Synge? Perhaps those who frequent the theatre or the cinema will, if pushed, remember that he wrote 'The Playboy of the Western World' and, if they are enthusiasts, may recall 'Riders to the Sea'. But what will they best recollect about 'Playboy'? Probably the fact that there were riots in theatres when the play was first performed.

Who was this John M Synge?

He was born on 16 April 1871 at Rathfarnham, then a village on the southern outskirts of Dublin. He was the fifth surviving child and the youngest. He was brought up in a family of Anglican clergy and his was a suffocating experience of childhood. The Synges were strict, evangelical and totally uncompromising and Sundays were austere. His relationship with his puritanical mother, especially after the death of his father when he was just a year old, was fraught. As he grew up, his views on the world were diametrically opposed to those of his mother. Yes he did go to church on Sundays, often more than once; yes he conformed, at least outwardly, to the directions of his mother and yes, he toed the religious line, or at least the family thought he did. But even from an early age, John ploughed his own furrow. He liked to read and spent time with Darwin's 'The Origin of Species'. He became interested in magic and mysticism and was soon straying from the religious 'straight and narrow'. And for a long time, his mother was blissfully unaware of her Johnny's predilections.

Although there were strains in their relationship on account of their differing views on faith and religious observance, Mrs Synge retained a soft spot for John throughout her life.

It should be noted that John was never a well child. As the years passed by he was regularly afflicted by ugly swellings on his neck. He was often poorly and under the weather. As a consequence his mother wouldn't allow him to attend the local schools and engaged tutors to teach the young boy. The fact that he did not have regular school friends did affect him significantly and, as a consequence, he was shy and reserved. His only outlet was spending time outdoors, especially with his county Wicklow family. He learned to play the violin and often accompanied his mother on the piano.

In 1888, when he was 17 years old, John enrolled at Trinity College. But he wasn't keen on his studies and was a very half-hearted student. He remained there for four years and his sole success in those years was to win 1st prize in Irish, a language then taught at the college and a subject he enjoyed.

Friends and acquaintances
In his twenties John spent time in Paris and was beginning to write poetry and plays although he was practically penniless like so many other Irish émigré playwrights and poets of the time. One of the first to meet John was none other than an equally impecunious WB Yeats, who was a few years his senior. The pair read and discussed the Irish poets of earlier years like Thomas Davis and John O'Leary. Yeats read some of the first poems that John had written and, as one came to expect of him, found the poems not quite up to his own exacting

standard. Yet Yeats did realise that, in JM Synge, Ireland could have found a literary gem. John met Maud Gonne at this time when Yeats (her ardent suitor) and he were spending so much time together. She impressed John, at least at the outset. Soon however, he broke his links with her because of her strident views on how to achieve Irish freedom – of which he strongly disapproved.

The Aran Islands – John Synge's Utopia

In 1898 John followed Yeats's advice and went to the Aran Islands, firstly to the main island, Inishmore, and then to the middle island, Inishmaan. There he found his spiritual and literary home. He was determined to speak Gaelic and found the best possible teacher, the half blind Old Mourteen. As a Protestant, John was a curiosity. And yet the older islanders remembered John's uncle, the Reverend Alexander Synge, who, believe it or not, had spent years on the islands trying to convert the locals. His mission began in 1851, not long after the Great Famine, and he stayed there for years. Whether or not he had any success is a matter of speculation although it hardly seems likely that he did succeed in making any or many converts. But at least he must have been relatively popular for, when the locals realised that John was the reverend's nephew, they quickly took to him. He spent most of his Aran time on Inishmaan and there he lodged with Pat MacDonagh, whose son, Martin, became his tutor. Fortunately the MacDonaghs spoke English which helped John as he was learning Gaelic.

It was during these frequent holidays on the Arans that John Synge's future plays were moulded and fashioned. The genesis for almost every one of his storylines came from these valuable times spent on the Arans – and this should always be remembered as his story progresses.

Coole Park and the Irish theatre

We should know that John Synge's life was to be a short one – he died when he was just 37 years old. It should then be remembered that his great works and plays, and his lasting influence on the Irish people, were squeezed into the last decade of his tragically short life.

During 1898, which was probably the most significant year of his life, John Synge was invited to call at Coole Park, the home of Lady Augusta Gregory. He appreciated that she was probably the most important person, and the driving force, in the burgeoning Irish theatre scene. He had been invited there, not initially by Lady Gregory herself, but by Willie Yeats who, by then, was a regular visitor. John became, almost without fully realising it, a member of what was to become the group of three who were to raise the profile of Irish works on the Irish stage with Irish actors and actresses performing them.

To begin with Lady Gregory considered Synge a kind of outsider and in truth she was probably a bit jealous of him. She too had spent some time on the Aran Islands gathering ideas for her own plays and learning Gaelic herself. Maybe she had not been quite so successful in this endeavour, so she took a little time to appreciate Synge's innate literary abilities. But she soon did and the two of them, along with Yeats, began setting up what was to become the Abbey theatre. Gradually Lady Gregory realised what a gem she, and Ireland, had discovered and so the troika set about awakening Ireland's literary soul. They had close contact with other poets and playwrights such as Edward Martyn, AE (George Russell) and Douglas Hyde. Initially John may have been uncomfortable in the surroundings of Coole Park but he was soon to see the place almost as a second home.

It is also interesting to note that Augusta Gregory, one of the very large family of Persses from nearby Roxborough, had had a similar type of upbringing as John Synge, for both had strict and austere parents – but both had skilfully managed to ease out of that uncompromising background and appreciate the true worth of the Irish people.

Wicklow – John's beloved native county

The Synges were Wicklow people and John had many cousins and family friends living in the Wicklow hills. John himself loved the outdoors and enjoyed rambles in the countryside with, for example, his cousin Florence Ross, on whom he had a crush in his early days. He often wondered why his mother did not approve of his talking to the local children whom she described as 'unsuitable', and yet as his life progressed, these were the very folk who were to feature in his popular plays.

A musical interlude

During his 20s John Synge had not yet achieved his life's goal – at least in terms of writing plays. He became very close to a girl called Cherie Matheson but, even in this relationship, he found barriers. She was from an exclusive Brethren family and this did not augur well for any future together. In the early 1890s, he decided that music might be an outlet and enrolled at the Royal School of Music in Dublin to study violin. He was encouraged by a cousin of his mother's to pursue this as a career and with her help, and his mother's reluctant agreement, he headed off for Oberwerth in Germany's Rhineland to study. It turned out to be a inspired choice of location; he was able to practise with the six young van Eicken sisters, the youngest of whom, Valeska, took his fancy; he was able to learn a new language and, above all, he was able to join in many little outdoor concerts in that beautiful part of Europe. Always in the background, though, loomed the shadowy figure of his mother who did not, of course, approve of her Johnny's career choice, but she did at least send him money to pursue his music studies. The violin might have been, as it were, a means of escaping his mother's pervading clutches, but John felt, deep down, that this was a mere stopgap in discovering the real John M Synge. Whilst in Germany he read some of the great German literary writers and he even started to write a few short plays in German. His mind was moving in a different direction for he knew that he did not want to further a musical career.

Time spent in Europe – to find a wife or to write plays?
John definitely changed his life's direction in 1894 when he returned home. He had certainly enjoyed his musical interlude in Germany with people whom he liked and loved. But in Dublin, albeit still close to his mother's overbearing influence, the young Synge finally decided that literature was his calling. He started once more to write some short plays but soon felt that life in Dublin was too restrictive

to pursue his newfound goal. He moved again to Paris, rather than going to London which might have seemed more sensible, and there quickly learned the language. He spent a lonely winter there attending talks, teaching English and falling in love with a lovely young Protestant French girl. However he still had feelings for Cherie back home and he even plucked up enough courage to propose to her. He didn't do it in the time-honoured way by going to see her, going down on his knee and asking her to be his wife. This might have worked but instead he wrote to her popping the question, only to be turned down and leaving him heartbroken.

Still practically penniless in the French capital, he once again appealed to his mother for funds and, as usual, after lecturing him about his lifestyle, she sent him sufficient money to keep his head above water. Now he headed off for Italy and immediately started to learn the language. We can see that he had a definite propensity for learning languages, having mastered German, French and now Italian in double quick time. He met more young women and it seemed pretty clear that he was obsessed with finding a wife.

John was now in his mid twenties and, with only a dozen or so years left to him, the question is often asked – when did he find time to nurture the genius that was John Millington Synge?

A return to Ireland – and the works of the genius Synge
John presented his first play to Lady Gregory on his first visit to Coole Park. We can imagine the scene – the young and very nervous Synge in the company of Yeats and his host. His play was rejected but Lady Gregory was astute enough to encourage John by saying that,

whilst the play did have merit, it would not suit the Irish theatre. Following this disappointment, John headed back to Inishmaan only to discover that an epidemic has broken out and a number of his friends were dead. There were even drownings from the boats that plied to and from the island. But from this tragedy burst forth the true genius of JM Synge. The year was 1901.

'Riders to the Sea' was his first success depicting, as it graphically did, the sadness and tragedy that had just hit Inishmaan. The play was an instant triumph. He was quickly spurred on to continue to relate life in all its starkness amongst the poor and unfortunate in the west of Ireland. He had seen it all; bouts of madness; deaths of young children; utter depression following the loss of family members which was all too common.

His 'Shadow of the Glen' was based around life in the impoverished parts of his own county of Wicklow where he knew the peasant folk and understood their tribulations. His friends in the Irish literary movement knew that they had found their prodigy, their mastermind. He went on to write 'The Tinker's Wedding', also centred around the people of Wicklow, their tinkers and their local fairs. Synge clearly knew where to find his material which, in Wicklow, was at his doorstep. He got on well with the people who became his plays' dramatis personae.

Generally speaking Lady Gregory loved his work although she thought 'The Tinker's Wedding' was too overtly critical of the Catholic Church. But his plays were now accepted and soon performed, except for 'The Tinker's Wedding' which was not performed in Dublin until 1971, the centenary of his birth.

Now that John Synge was so popular, his works desperately needed the appropriate actors and actresses to play the parts. The Fay brothers were the most talented actors and so they were given leading roles in his plays. Finding actresses was a little more difficult although Mary Walker was to become one of the best actresses to speak exactly as the islanders of Inishmaan spoke.

Opposition to his plays

Nothing of course was ever straightforward. The Synge plays were performed to his complete satisfaction but there were those in the world outside of the theatre who had other views, many of them negative. Reports in the newspapers, especially after the early performances of 'Shadow', were unhelpful and denigrating. Many had found the play distasteful and an offence to the peasant people of Ireland. Supposed luminaries such as Arthur Griffith, Maud Gonne and even James Connolly were disgusted by the portrayal of the characters in his play. Thankfully many others would come to his defence like WB Yeats's father, John, and WB Yeats himself. They condemned those critics for their complete ignorance of the lives of those depicted in Synge's play and they declared their total and unequivocal support for the fair and decent – and talented - man that John Synge was. He was not an ogre; he was a man of brilliance.

'Riders to the Sea', performed after 'Shadow', also evoked venom but by now those who should have known better now admitted that the storylines behind Synge's plays showed merit. His former critics realised that the content of these plays did in fact depict real life in

Ireland in all its starkness and brutal reality. This was truly Synge's forte; this was Synge's gift to the Irish theatre.

Bad health again intervenes – but so do fame and fortune

We must never forget that John Synge was a sick young man. He suffered from grotesque swellings and thought he had TB. He moved backwards and forwards between Dublin and London even when he was feeling decidedly under the weather. His plays were receiving good reviews in London. But they needed to find their own theatre and in 1904 Willie Fay found the old Mechanics' Institute which was to become the Abbey Theatre. They now had their home but they also needed money to finance it. Lady Gregory, using her skills of persuasion and influence, found Annie Horniman, a wealthy woman who wanted to help the burgeoning theatre. Lady Gregory, during these years, had to keep a balance between her innate nationalism and the need to keep in with her well-to-do gentry friends to keep the Abbey going.

John had written another play 'The Well of the Saints' which was also set in Wicklow and soon afterwards he visited the Mullet peninsula in west Mayo for the first time and here he quickly found material for yet another play.

For the first time in his life John became the focus of attention in Dublin. The days of negativity about his brilliant plays had now passed and he was even beginning to cut a dash in Dublin society. Young men and women were flocking to be auditioned at the Abbey to be a part of his ever-popular plays. The best known of these star finds were Sara and Molly Allgood and, before long, the 17-year-old

Molly had fallen for the playwright who, by 1905, was 34. In these days, too, John showed his firmness when he insisted on his actors and actresses depicting their roles exactly as he had written them. The Fay brothers, by now legends in their own right, commended Synge on his plays and on the way he wanted them acted. They thought that 'The Well' was his best play yet.

Synge depicted life in his plays as it really was, tough and hard. He never wrote a play which was overly coloured just to make the audience like it. His theatre audiences began to appreciate how essential it was to be 'drawn into' his productions so that they would understand his plots. Another clever aspect of his plays was the use of only minimal movement on the stage by the actors and actresses. This was also a new trend, and one much admired by the literary cognoscenti. Lady Gregory and Willie Yeats knew that they had found a true genius and the Abbey went from strength to strength. The Synge masterpieces were already being translated into French and German, another sure sign of their worth.

A new friendship and visits to yet more places

At this crucial stage in Synge's career, he met up with Willie Yeats's younger brother, Jack, who was an artist, but not as well known in his field as he should have been. He was an outstanding painter but, because of his rather quiet personality, he rarely held exhibitions and never seemed to attract sufficient commissions. John Synge liked him a lot and they were soon travelling all over the west of Ireland, visiting places such as the Mullet peninsula and Connemara. Synge thought up the new stories and Yeats painted the illustrations. They were a well-matched pair.

Synge then went to visit the Blasket islands off the Kerry coast. He was well received there by the islanders and their king and it proved to be an ideal location for yet another play which was based on the fact that the Blasket folk were bellicose and belligerent. This was a side of the native Irish that Synge had never seen before. He was, of course, saddened by the fact that the young people from the island were leaving in their droves for a new life in America.

Trouble at the Abbey – and more problems with his health

But when he returned to Dublin after his wanderings in the west, Synge encountered trouble at the Abbey. The acting staff and Lady Gregory and Willie Yeats were not seeing eye to eye with each other and some of the better actresses were leaving. Worse still, many of their patrons, and even eventually Annie Horniman, began to desert the theatre. The Abbey was on a knife's edge. But the troika were not going to be put off and took a firm stance, regardless of what was happening around them, to withdraw the veto right from the acting staff. This was a brave decision especially in the circumstances, but they ploughed on and the theatre's fortunes began to change. For the 1906 season, Synge's play 'Riders to the Sea' was to be included.

Synge was happy with the plans for the new year but, once more, problems with his fragile health intervened. Everyone was concerned, yet John decided to carry on regardless. What was driving him was his love for Molly Allgood. A true romance blossomed and he quickly agreed to act in his 'Riders' opposite Molly who had a leading role.

They travelled with the company to various Irish provincial towns and also to a number of British cities. It was a stressful and extremely busy time, but John's love for Molly became an infatuation and even an embarrassment to Lady Gregory and to their actor friends. In truth John knew that his time was short and he wanted to make the most of what time he had left. In many ways he did not care what others thought of his romance, he just wanted to make the most of it.

'Playboy of the Western World'

And so, in 1907, was John Synge's greatest work completed. It was to be his last and the one remembered best of all. It is played throughout the world to this very day and yet, at the time, when he was at the peak of his literary and personal artistic success, he was to face his fiercest critics, his audiences. There were riots when the play was first performed at the Abbey; there was opposition in the press about his representation of the people of the Mullet where sprang the genesis of the work. Even though he was in relatively poor health, John still had to go out and face the audiences. He had to stand on the stage and tell them, who knew nothing of the west of Ireland folk, that the play was an accurate depiction of life there. There was trouble aplenty not only with the storyline itself, but with the use of words and the description of emotions that were not what the regular audiences were used to hearing. The most infamous word used in this play was 'shift', a word for a woman's undergarment. This word was perfectly understood by everyone in the theatre; this word was used within the confines of their own homes; but how dare this word be used in public and on a stage in a play by a man reputed to be the best playwright in the country. The men and the women in the audience were just being hypocritical and continued to expect happy endings to every show they attended at a theatre. Reality was different and it was John Millington Synge who had the courage and perspicacity to say it.

There were, in the days and weeks after the first performances, many discussions about the merits of this Synge play. Lady Gregory knew that he was the best Ireland had produced and so she and Yeats and others encouraged these discourses. Why did Synge use particular words and phrases? Why did he write lines and words that actors and actresses would have difficulty in reciting? The answer really is in his brilliance – he was a man before his time and as we know, he did not live long enough to write more such searching works.

Even the use of the word 'playboy', in the context of an Irish play, was hard to understand. It was not a word in general use anywhere in Ireland; it was difficult to translate into other languages; it was perhaps Synge's own clever way of making Irish audiences move forward. It is hard to believe that this play also contained a good deal of comedy and many romantic interludes, with obvious allusions to his love for Molly Allgood. 'Playboy' was a complex work but, as the years progressed after the death of its writer, it became a definite Irish masterpiece and acknowledged as such by the great and the good in the literary world and the wise and the profound in the theatre-going public. Campaigns continued to oppose 'Playboy'. Those who spoke out against the production included Arthur Griffith and even Patrick Pearse. When the play arrived in America there were riots there as well although it is hard to understand what the Americans would have really known about life in the raw in rural western Ireland. Maybe someone, or the press, had just told them to protest regardless.

Nearing the end

Whilst John was pleased that, despite the ructions surrounding the production, the play went on from strength to strength. But he wanted to move on to different themes and he decided to write about the epic story of Deirdre. He started to write 'Deirdre of the Sorrows' which certainly would be a contrast – and a stark one at that – from the life of a peasant to that of a very regal queen. He was exhausted and needed a break from the Abbey and the controversy surrounding 'Playboy'. He and Molly spent time in his beloved Wicklow although Molly was unwell herself and John's condition was clearly deteriorating. He had an operation on a large swelling on his neck and was generally feeling pretty miserable. The only positive note was that Molly had agreed to marry him and all he wanted was to be well enough to look forward to his wedding.

In the meantime another American tour had been arranged but 'Playboy' was not to be included in the programme. He was angry with Lady Gregory and Willie Yeats for agreeing to this and he felt that they had let him down. He threatened to resign his Abbey directorship but, in the end, stayed put.

By the early months of 1908 he was told that he had cancer – Hodgkin's disease. The diagnosis was not good and by April the associated tumour was inoperable. The family and his friends now realised how ill he was. He spent more time in Wicklow along with Molly and was well enough for them to walk in the glens. John decided to visit Germany again to see his friends in Oberwerth and, when he was there, he heard of the death of his mother. To make matters worse, he was not well enough to travel home for her funeral. He eventually returned home early in 1909 and needed to enter a nursing home in March. There he died on 24 March 1909, aged just 37. He was buried in a family grave where two of his aunts had been interred. It was a small and private ceremony with just a few of his family and friends from the Abbey in attendance, although Molly herself stayed away, too grief stricken to attend. It seemed a sorry end for one of Ireland's literary giants, without even having his own grave.

What then have we to say about this true genius of the Irish theatre?

John M Synge was a man ahead of his time. He was probably the first Irish playwright to live with, get to know and fully appreciate the people about whom he wrote. The native Irish speakers in the places he visited - the Arans, the Blaskets and the Mullet peninsula - admired Synge and even considered him one of their own. His relations with his closest friends like Augusta Gregory and Willie Yeats were usually good for they realised he had been a godsend to them. Relations with his overprotective and evangelical mother were sometimes strained but, in general terms, they got on tolerably well as the years progressed. The contemporary he got on with best was perhaps Jack Yeats for he seemed to fully understand him.

As the twentieth century moved forward, other playwrights came to the fore – Sean O'Casey and Samuel Beckett. But the name which stands out is that of JM Synge. He surely pulled the theatre-going Irish public, kicking and screaming, to savour, enjoy and, above all, understand, the true worth of a play set in rural Ireland – let us continue to be grateful for the life of John Millington Synge.

Curious for more?

I can recommend these books for further reading:

Carpenter, Andrew (ed), *My Uncle John – Edward Stephens's Life of J. M. Synge*, London, Oxford University Press, 1974.

Kiely, David. M., *John Millington Synge – a Biography*, Dublin, Gill & Macmillan, 1994.

McCormack, W. J., *Fool of the Family – a Life of J. M. Synge*, London, Weidenfeld & Nicolson, 2000.

For books that aren't in common circulation I may be able to source them for you. Email me at clive.scoular@gmail.com or check out my website – *clivescoular.com*.

Running Guns to Ireland

*Molly Childers, left, and Mary Spring Rice
aboard the* Asgard

GUN RUNNING TO Ireland sounds almost unbelievable – but it did happen, both in Ulster and in Howth in county Dublin. Both incidents took place in 1914, the year of the outbreak of the Great War. There were, as in all such dramatic episodes, two significant figures and the name associated with Ulster was Frederick Crawford and with Howth, Erskine Childers. And so it would be wise to tell the stories of these two intrepid, courageous and – some would say – reckless men up to the time of their involvement in the gun running of 1914.

Fred Crawford was born in Belfast in 1861 into a stolid Methodist family and, although a worthy unionist, did have descendants who had fought against the British establishment in the 1798 rebellion where upwards of 30,000 people were killed. He worked as an engineer and spent time in Australia before returning home and enlisting in the British army to fight in the Boer War. As a lifelong unionist he joined the Ulster Unionist Council in 1911 and was the man who organised all the stewards and marshals at Belfast City Hall on 28 September 1912 when the Ulster Covenant was signed. He allegedly signed the document in his own blood as a number of others were supposed to have done. Whether or not this is true, it does make a good story. He went on to fight in the Great War and lead a most interesting and active life until his death, at age 91, in 1952.

Erskine Childers was the archetypal English gentleman who, although born in England, spent much of his childhood with his cousins in county Wicklow after the death of his parents. He fought for king and country in both the Boer and the Great Wars and was decorated for his bravery. He became an author of note and his first novel, 'The Riddle of the Sands', is still being republished to the present day. After the First World War, and after considerable heart searching, he espoused the Irish cause and, like most zealous converts, he nevermore wavered from his goal of separating Ireland from the British Empire by means of physical force. When the time came in 1914 to raise the tempo, it was Childers who put his neck on the line and not only offered to arrange to purchase illegal arms for the Irish Volunteers but also to go in his own yacht to bring them to Ireland. He died a martyr's death in 1922 during the Irish Civil War.

The Ulster Gun Running

The talk of Home Rule was on everyone's lips for many years before the turn of the twentieth century. At the beginning, of course, the determination was to move to Irish independence by constitutional means and this was the tack taken, in the first instance, by Charles Stewart Parnell and by John Redmond. When the Liberals were in power in Westminster, they, along with the 80 or so Irish Parliamentary Party MPs, pressed hard for Home Rule. Although the first and second Home Rule Bills of 1886 and 1893 failed to get past the House of Lords, the situation was greatly changed with the introduction of the Parliament Act in 1912 which ensured that the Upper House could not baulk acts passed by the Lower House on more than three occasions. For the Ulster Unionists, who would not countenance a separation from the United Kingdom under any circumstances, the situation was dire. They needed to act – but how?

Ulster's saviour was none other than Fred Crawford. He was a man of action. In the early 1890s, when the Liberals with the Irish Party (though by now somewhat disorganised after the death of Parnell in 1891) were in power, the likelihood of Irish independence did appear reasonably likely. Crawford saw the writing on the wall and started on what I would call his life's work to preserve the Union – the illegal importation of arms into Ulster. He looked around and saw the Unionists burying their heads in the sand. The Tories had returned to power in 1895, which meant the pressure for separation had, at least temporarily, receded. And so they laid back on their laurels. Crawford took up the cudgels and did his best to bully his unionist friends out of their false sense of security. They didn't listen so he took matters into his own hands. In 1906 he put an advertisement in the papers of a number of European countries seeking second hand rifles and ammunition. Imagine someone reading this in, say, Belgium or Germany – would anyone take this request seriously? Crawford had even given the name of a fictitious person at the Ulster Club in Belfast as the respondent. He knew he was likely to incur the wrath of the Unionist hierarchy and he certainly did when a number of positive replies came rolling in. He was sacked from a post he held in Belfast but Crawford minded not a jot. He already had procured some arms, which he immediately showed to the Ulster Unionist Council and their lily-livered members who quaked at the sight of guns and rifles in the hallowed sanctuary of their headquarters. Many of them resigned – good riddance thought Crawford.

However the remainder of the Council authorised Crawford to buy more weapons and he managed, sometimes successfully and sometimes not, to bring them in. It may seem strange to say that it was not actually illegal to import arms into Ireland although the government, after seizing some small consignments, did start to clamp down on this nefarious activity. Debates in the House of Commons, often centring on Irish matters of course, were now discussing how to counter any further importation of illegal arms.

By 1911 Ireland was once again in turmoil with the Nationalists wanting complete freedom from Westminster and the Unionists not wanting any severance from the United Kingdom. Crawford was now in his element. He made a number of daring proposals to both James Craig and Edward Carson. He told them he had a friend in Hamburg who could be relied upon to sell the Unionists arms. Crawford knew that these leaders were in two minds about his audacious plans. Would they agree or would they, like so many other weak-willed Unionists, prefer not to proceed?

Whilst the wavering was going on, Crawford travelled to Germany where he purchased 15,000 Austrian and 5,000 German rifles with a great deal of ammunition. He spent the remarkable sum of £70,000 on the weapons and, upon hearing what had been done on their behalf, the majority of the Unionists finally, if still a little reluctantly, approved. The Ulster Volunteer Force was now well armed.

Putting the plan into effect

We can only imagine how the Ulster Unionist Council members felt at their meeting after they heard of the arms purchase. One of their number had used their money to buy arms; one of their number had ridden roughshod over their previous decisions to go carefully over the matter of bringing in arms and one of their number had put their esteemed leader, Sir Edward Carson, in the horns of a dilemma. But even the bold and intrepid Crawford had to be absolutely sure he had Carson's permission to go ahead. So he visited him in London on his way to the continent. Carson hemmed and hawed but, in the end, gave in and agreed that Crawford should proceed. He even told Crawford that he would take any of the consequences, including the prospect of a prison sentence, and leave Crawford in the clear.

With his leader's approval ringing in his ears, Crawford set off to his friend Bruno Spiro in Hamburg. He approved the consignment of arms and ammunition but insisted that the weapons should be wrapped in bundles of five rifles with the requisite ammunition in each bundle. This was to make the unloading and collection in Ireland all the easier – this was, in truth, a stroke of genius. Thus it meant that those picking up the weapons for the various towns and villages could simply ask for the agreed number of bundles, load them into their cars and drive off to their home place.

Crawford now owned the guns but he had to arrange for them to be brought home. This was yet another complicated matter made easy by Crawford's innate genius. The first thing he needed was a ship on which to transport the weapons – so off he went to Bergen and decided on one called the *Fanny*. It cost him the princely sum of £2,000. He needed a captain who could take the ship to Ireland so he engaged a man called Falke, who was a Norwegian, to take command and, as he would still be technically the owner of the ship, it could proceed under the Norwegian flag through the continental waterways without arousing any suspicion. But first Crawford needed to transport the guns from Hamburg to the North Sea, so he hired two lighters and brought his guns through the Kiel Canal. There he rendezvoused with Captain Falke, transferred the guns to the *Fanny* and headed for Ireland. All did not go absolutely smoothly but a testing interview with an inquisitive port official was successfully concluded. They were on their way.

But like all such exciting adventure stories, there were still many hurdles to cross and difficulties to overcome. Originally they were intending to go north to Iceland and then come round the north west coast of Scotland but the plan was changed, presumably on the whim of the Norwegian captain and not by the daring Fred Crawford. They sailed through the English Channel which was certainly not the safest route for a ship loaded with illegal arms. It seems that Crawford became ill on board ship and the captain wanted to land him somewhere in England for treatment. Crawford declined the proposal and insisted that the ship sail on. They arrived at Lundy Island in the Bristol Channel. Crawford was taken ashore at Tenby and returned to Belfast to have another meeting with Carson and Craig. To further complicate matters, it was decided that the *Fanny* should not bring the arms home and that another ship should be bought to undertake the mission. The *Clydevalley* - then renamed the *Mountjoy* - was bought in Glasgow and sailed to Lundy Island to have the assignment transferred aboard.

The guns arrive

Anyone with some knowledge of this most audacious of incidents in Ireland's history will tell you that the Ulster Volunteers' guns were landed at Larne. This is true, but is not the whole story. The *Mountjoy* arrived at Larne harbour late on the night of 24 April 1914 (exactly two years before the outbreak of the 1916 Easter Rising as it so happens). The quayside was eerily silent with neat rows of cars lined up close to the ship. With military precision the bundles of weapons were brought off the ship by the sailors who simply asked each driver for the number required for their own town or village – it went something like this – name and destination please – Killyleagh, county Down, ten bundles – agreed as per my list – here they are – and off they drove. And so it continued until all the requisite bundles had been unloaded and despatched. But were the police and customs officials not around to thwart their plans? They were not because earlier in the evening, as per instructions from Belfast Unionist HQ, they had been 'confined to their barracks and offices' by members of 'unionist officialdom'. In other plain words, their premises had been entered by armed men, who then held the policemen and customs men captive until after the operation was over. Telephone communications were also severed thus preventing news of the arrival of the ship being broadcast. It is interesting to note that at that time there were just under 1,000 cars registered in the entire Belfast/Antrim area and over half of all of these vehicles took part in the operation. The guns had been run and landed without incident.

But there is another part of the story which is largely unknown. Yes, guns were run to Larne but part of the *Mountjoy*'s consignment was transferred to two smaller ships which drew alongside. These little boats, in the early hours of the 25th, set sail for Bangor and Donaghadee where they were unloaded and the bundles taken to locations on the Ards peninsula and to Newtownards and Comber. The man in charge of the Donaghadee landings was none other than James Craig himself assisted by members of the Andrews family (amongst whose number was a future Prime Minister of Northern Ireland and the designer of the ill-fated *Titanic*).

Where were the rest of the government officials when they belatedly heard of the gun running? There had been rumours of such a plot to bring in arms illegally and the obvious place to land them was surely at Belfast harbour somewhere. But, as the saying goes, Crawford had this covered. He knew that they would be expected to land at the biggest port and so he sent a decoy vessel, *Balmerino*, into Belfast that evening. There were on board many suspicious parcels and boxes which the officials gleefully unpacked assuming that they had foiled this dastardly plot. They searched and searched; they ripped open parcel after parcel; they prised apart box after box. But all to no avail as they soon realised that they had been duped. The ruse had worked and whilst the officials searched the boat in Belfast, the guns were being unloaded and dispersed without incident at Larne, Bangor and Donaghadee.

The Ulster Unionists and the Ulster Volunteers now had their guns – what would they now do with them? This is a story for another day although it must be admitted that this tale of derring-do would do well on the silver screen. I ask you – why not make a film of this most exciting, audacious and thrilling episode in our country's history?

The Howth Gun Running

The Ulster Volunteers were well organised, well financed, great in numbers and keen to arm. In contrast, the Irish Volunteers were enthusiastic, very poorly financed, greater in numbers than the Ulstermen and not that keen to arm. These, in my estimation, are the bare facts. The northern volunteers, though oftentimes marching with replica wooden rifles, knew what they needed and, by virtue of the indomitable character of Fred Crawford, went ahead and purchased a veritable fearsome arsenal. They had more than sufficient funds to buy their guns and the determination to use them if necessary. The southern Volunteers looked to the north and saw the gritty resolve of the Ulstermen and women. But they were desperately short of funds and the means by which to find weapons. A committee of the Irish Volunteers was set up mainly manned by a number of Anglo Irish men and women. The leading lights were Erskine Childers and his American born wife, Molly, and Darrell Figgis. They agreed that the Irish Volunteers needed to purchase arms and find the money to buy them. They also urgently wanted a ship to transport whatever guns they were able to purchase on the continent.

Childers was asked to find a vessel on which to transport their haul and he was pleased to assist. He heard of a boat based at Foynes on the Shannon but, having seen it, realised that it needed too many repairs and would therefore cost more than their committee could afford and so was not purchased. He returned to Dublin and, after consultation with his wife, decided to offer his own yacht, *Asgard*, which had been a wedding present from Molly's father. Another yacht belonging to Conor O'Brien called the *Kelpie* was offered as an additional craft.

Darrell Figgis then set out for Hamburg on a mission – to buy as many weapons as could be afforded. Childers accompanied Figgis, firstly to Liege in Belgium where the guns on offer were too expensive and then to Hamburg where the prospective supplier, Moritz Magnus, appeared suspicious. In the end 1,500 guns and 26,000 rounds of ammunition were sold to the Irishmen after they implied that the guns were destined for Mexico and the deception seemed to work. They had their guns although the sum of £1,523 did not buy as many as they would have wanted and what they did purchase were of poor quality – and that was to put it mildly – they had, after all, only cost £1 each. It seems they were of Franco-Prussian War (1870) vintage and much of the ammunition sold with the weapons was of the wrong calibre.

However Figgis and Childers had fulfilled their aim although they now had to get the arms back to Ireland without being intercepted by British gunboats travelling up and down the English Channel. They engaged a tug to take the guns to a lighthouse off the Dutch coast where the *Kelpie* and the *Asgard* rendezvoused with the tug. The *Kelpie* was supposed to be loaded with half the haul – i.e. 750 guns – but could only take 600. This left the *Asgard* to take 900 on board. This was just a cruising yacht and certainly not built to be filled with rifles and ammunition. When all the guns were on board there was no room to move, sleep or even to prepare meals. The entire vessel was choked to the gunnels with the weapons. Those on the yacht, which included Molly Childers and her friend, Mary Spring Rice, were squashed into any available corner while the boat made slow progress. *Asgard* must have attracted much suspicion being, as it was, extremely low in the water. The tug which had been hired was now required to tow the *Asgard* to Dover which would have caused more suspicious glances.

In the end, however, the boat managed to make its way to Howth harbour, just north of Dublin. It had been expected and a motorboat had been assigned to go out to meet the *Asgard* and accompany it into the harbour. But when they arrived on 26 July 1914, there was no sign of the motorboat so Childers just decided to sail into the harbour. As luck would have it, around 800 Volunteers and 100 Fianna Scouts were on the quayside to meet the boat and the guns were simply thrown up to the waiting men. Each man grabbed a gun and headed off for the city. The authorities and police were slow in reacting to what was clearly an illegal importation of arms and were not able to arrest many of the Volunteers or to capture many of the weapons. In fact just about two dozen of the rifles fell into their hands.

Childers and his crew had, however, completed their task – they had brought in arms for the Irish Volunteers. The remaining guns being brought by the *Kelpie* had been transferred to Sir Thomas Myles's steam yacht, *Chotah*, and they were landed a week later at Kilcoole in county Wicklow, a small seaside village south of Dublin.

It is now up to you to assess the worth of the weapons brought in by the Ulster and the Irish Volunteers. The statistics do make stark reading. £70,000 for the Ulstermen compared with just over £1,500 for the southern Volunteers.

Curious for more?

I can recommend these books for further reading:

Crawford, Fred, *Guns for Ulster*.

Martin, F.X., *The Howth Gun Running*, Dublin, Merrion Press, 2014.

For books that aren't in common circulation I may be able to source them for you. Email me at clive.scoular@gmail.com or check out my website – *clivescoular.com*.

The Black and Tans

Auxiliaries preparing for action

I F THE TERM 'Black and Tans' was heard in Ireland before 1920, most people would not have had a clue what was being spoken about, but if there were hunting folk in the company they would immediately have associated the name with a world famous pack of foxhounds from county Limerick in the south west of Ireland.

The name took on an altogether different connotation in 1920. By this time in Ireland's fraught history, the Irish War of Independence, or the Anglo Irish War, was being fought throughout the country. But these names were quickly forgotten because everyone now called the conflict the Black and Tan War. It did not mean, however, that packs of wild dogs were attacking the British Crown forces – it meant that a new force had arrived in Ireland from Britain to put down an ever-problematic rebellion. These were young men who had returned from service in the First World War; these were soldiers who, unlike so many of their pals, had actually survived that conflict; these were men who fully expected to find work 'fit for heroes' after their exemplary conduct and bravery on the Western front. But they were to be cruelly disappointed. There were no jobs and rather than being seen as conquering heroes they were cruelly cast aside. In many cases they were completely ignored – and by those whose very lives had been saved by their courage and gallantry.

And so these young men looked for work wherever it was to be found. When they saw advertisements in the British newspapers looking for part time soldiers 'to face a rough and dangerous task' to help quell the uprising in Ireland, many quickly applied and were hired. They were offered the princely sum of 10/- (50p) per week with board and lodgings included. After some minimal training these men found themselves in a country which very few of them had ever visited before and this meant difficulties from the start. Upon arrival they were kitted out in their uniforms and, rather than traditional British army ones, they were presented with khaki coloured trousers and dark blue tunics and caps. Looking at each other they wondered why the strange get up. It was simple – the authorities didn't have enough full uniforms to give to their new recruits. And so, as you've probably already guessed, they at once became known as the 'Black and Tans'. Little did they know at the time that this name would quickly become synonymous with an ill-disciplined and reckless force. Their commanding officer, who seemingly was not much looking forward to his posting, was Sir Nevil McCready, a highly decorated and able soldier. He had his work cut out for him and he knew it.

Many of these new recruits found themselves posted to rural areas of county Cork, for example. No one had told them anything about Ireland, far less about what they were expected to do in the hills and towns of a county whose name most of them had never heard before. They were also upset when they read some of the local newspapers announcing their arrival. 'These demoralised and discontented men were the sweepings of English jails' were now loose on the streets of Ireland. They certainly were not as described for, as we already know, most of them were brave soldiers who had survived the Great War – but there was little they could do to refute these false claims. Yet they had to get on with their job of trying to calm the Irish. It looked like a pretty difficult job – and so it was to prove.

The state of Ireland in 1920

For the army and civil authorities in Ireland in early 1920, life was hard and almost intolerable. British power was beginning to break down and the gap was being filled, in many cases extremely competently, by the local Sinn Fein personnel. Law and order, British style, was breaking down and throughout the country police barracks and courthouses were being attacked and burned down. The Sinn Feiners themselves were taking over the running of the country with their own courts and police force. And the remarkable thing was that they were making a much better fist of it than had the British. There are many stories told of members of the Irish gentry taking thorny problems to these illegal courts and receiving fair and decent outcomes – and often in double quick time.

In March 1920 the Lord Mayor of Cork, Tomas MacCurtain, was assassinated on his own doorstep. The Black and Tans, newly arrived of course, were immediately accused of this dastardly deed. They denied the charge but no one believed them. It later transpired that Royal Irish Constabulary men had shot the mayor. This fact did little to improve the already low standing of the new force. But as the year passed on the Black and Tans were involved in many unsavoury incidents. They were still just as ignorant of what was going on around them and the surroundings in which they found themselves.

The arrival of the 'Auxies'

The authorities felt that they needed yet more men to complement their already overworked force. There still were the two police forces in Ireland, it should be remembered, the Royal Irish Constabulary and the Dublin Metropolitan Police, but vast numbers of them were resigning their posts. It was ever more difficult to be a policeman in Ireland in the middle of its internecine struggle. More senior men were needed – and urgently. Yet more adverts were placed in English papers for a force to be called 'The Auxiliary Division of the RIC', or the 'Auxies', and to these posts were attracted men who had held officer rank during the Great War. They were to be paid £1.00 per week, twice the rate of their juniors in the Black and Tans. Soon then these former officers landed in Ireland, just as ill informed of the people and their surroundings as the men in the Black and Tans. This group of men was not to find popularity in the country, rather they became even more despised than the lower ranks.

Life in a rural Irish county

For the Black and Tans garrisoned in county Cork, life was restrictive, to say the least. After spending their days in the countryside pursuing the IRA, sometimes successfully but more often without anything to show for their efforts, they had to retire to their barracks. There was never any opportunity to go to the local public houses or other places of entertainment for they were decidedly personae non gratae amongst the civilian population. They were hemmed in and more and more bored and unhappy and there was always an air of suspense.

When they occasionally did get out, they quickly got drunk and caused yet more disruption. It was a 'no win' situation for them.

County Cork was difficult terrain for these men but quite the opposite for the locals who knew all the right places to ambush the soldiers when they drove along in their armoured cars and open lorries. There were many killed in these sharp encounters and the IRA felt they held the upper hand. The Black and Tans would often have agreed although they did, as they saw it, have some success in capturing and shooting some of their ambushers. The name on their lips as the man everyone wanted in custody was that of Michael Collins, who was a native of the county although he rarely was to be found there – apart from when he would have surreptitiously called with his family near their home outside Clonakilty. It is hardly surprising that he was dubbed 'The Scarlet Pimpernel' or, by others, 'Robin Hood'.

Many of the atrocities carried out by the Crown forces were not in fact the work of the Black and Tans. Whilst they did of course inflict many deaths and injuries, lots of these incidents ought to have been attributed to the local police.

Burnings, killings and other outrages

Towards the end of 1920 life throughout Ireland, and particularly in places like county Cork, became unbearable both for the local population and for the police and army, the Black and Tans and the Auxies. There were attacks and reprisals, burnings and shootings. By September 54 policemen and 12 soldiers had been killed and over thirty courthouses burned and hundreds of cases of arson. Even coastguard stations were being raided. By now many of the 'Big Houses' of Ireland were being set alight causing, as is often forgotten, greater unemployment as lots of the locals worked on the gentry estates.

The Lord Mayor of Cork who had succeeded Tomas MacCurtain, Terence McSwiney, was arrested and immediately went on a hunger strike. He died after 75 days causing yet more pain and disruption all over the country and this was followed by the hanging of a young man called Kevin Barry. When Michael Collins ordered the assassination of a number of British agents on 21 November 1920, the British sent armoured cars into Croke Park where a football match was being played. Fourteen civilians were killed, including one of the players. In the succeeding days a number of towns throughout Ireland like Ennistymon, Lahinch and Trim were sacked and large areas burned to the ground. The blame fell upon the Black and Tans and the Auxiliaries; they were feared and revenge for their dreadful acts was demanded. On 28 November 1920, seventeen of eighteen Auxies travelling through county Cork were ambushed and killed at Kilmichael. Even worse was to follow when, on the night of 11 December, the main street of the city of Cork was maliciously set on fire by the Auxies and, as the city burned, members of the Black and Tans were to be seen looting the fine shops of the street. The hated force became even more despised and recriminations were exacted.

The year 1921 was to be even more horrific. At Easter, in a coordinated and simultaneous operation, the IRA fired 182 vacated police stations and courthouses. It is hard to imagine the chaos and mayhem caused by this attack. There was little that the Black and

Tans, the Auxies or the RIC could do. One can only wonder how none of the Crown forces, nearly 30,000 of them, were on hand to prevent this act of abject vandalism. It almost looked like a scorched earth policy being perpetrated by the IRA on behalf of the majority of the people of Ireland.

What was the reaction at Westminster?

Attention at Westminster was being regularly diverted in order that MPs could discuss the troubled times in Ireland. They could have done without these preoccupations but the news from across the Irish Sea always seemed negative. The House was debating the Government of Ireland Act which, to many, was really the Fourth Home Rule Bill. But the act meant a division of the country with the six north eastern counties becoming Northern Ireland and the remaining 26 becoming 'southern Ireland', soon, after partition, to become the Irish Free State. And yet in the midst of these debates the news of the atrocities carried out by the Black and Tans and the IRA were ever to the fore. The MPs wanted one thing for Ireland – and that was a peaceful solution to the conflict.

There is a sobering statistic about those executed by the state. In the heat of the battle, from autumn 1920 until the summer of 1921 the British authorities put to death 24 Republicans for criminal acts leading to the death penalty. During the Civil War which took place immediately after partition, 77 so called anti-Treaty Irishmen were put to death by legislation of the new state's making. This is something that we, as Irishmen from either the north or the south, ought never to forget.

In the end an election was held in both parts of the newly divided country with some startling results. In the south Republicans/ Sinn Feiners won 124 seats, all or most of them unopposed. For the northern parliament, out of 52 seats, Unionists won 40 and twelve were won by Republicans amongst whom, it may be surprising to relate, included Eamon de Valera, Arthur Griffith and that most shadowy figure of all, Michael Collins. If today people were asked the question 'true or false' if these three men had been elected to a northern parliament, I think the answer would almost certainly be 'false'.

The War of Independence eventually stopped in the summer of 1921 when King George V visited Belfast and made a conciliatory speech appealing to the warring sides to sign a truce. And it worked – fighting ceased on 11 July that year.

And what of the Black and Tans?

They just wanted to go home. They had become to so many, both in Great Britain and in Ireland, a source of enmity and even hatred and so the end of the war allowed them to return to their homes across the Irish Sea.

But like it or not, the Black and Tans had made a marked, if controversial, contribution to the history of Ireland.

Curious for more?

I can recommend these books for further reading:

Bennett, Richard, *The Black and Tans*, London, Edward Hulton, 1959.

Dwyer, T. Ryle, *Tans, Terror and Troubles – Kerry's Real Fighting Story 1913 – 23*, Cork, Mercier Press, 2001.

For books that aren't in common circulation I may be able to source them for you. Email me at clive.scoular@gmail.com or check out my website – *clivescoular.com*.

The Great Flu 1918 - 1919

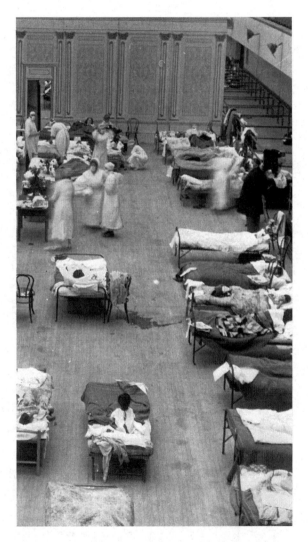

Red Cross nurses tend to flu patients in temporary wards set up inside an auditorium in America. Scenes like this were replicated worldwide.

THE SIMPLE AND most shocking fact is that perhaps twice as many people were killed in a period of less than twelve months in this outbreak of flu than were killed during the entire four years of the Great War. There were upwards of 20 million who lost their lives in the war but maybe as many as 50 million who fell victim to this pestilence, which arrived in the summer of 1918 and departed in the spring of 1919. These are the grim statistics and the tragic facts of a pestilence either completely unknown or totally forgotten by succeeding generations.

This flu broke out in absolutely every part of the world, even in the Arctic Circle. There are horrific stories of piles of unburied bodies being shovelled up in the streets of Indian cities and in the heart of the continent of Africa. In Ireland itself, during the election which followed the Great War at the end of 1918, election candidates, rather than engaging in the rough and tumble of their campaign, were witnessing nothing but funeral processions and tales of how difficult it was to find coffins and even enough plots in which to bury the dead of the plague. The situation in Ireland at the time of the opening of the First Dail in January 1919 was particularly bad and many of the elected TDs were unable to take their places owing to being struck down by the flu. Many men in prison and even many 'on the run' at this pivotal time in Ireland's history, suffered the same fate. And some of them actually died.

In Ireland over 20,000 people died of the flu and throughout Great Britain another 200,000. There was no doubt that this pandemic was far worse than even the Black Plague of 1348. In truth it wreaked much more havoc than did the Great Famine in the late 1840s.

What was this flu and how did it affect its victims?

People were struck down suddenly and without warning. Blood started to flow from every orifice of the body and skin became blue in colour due to lack of blood. Autopsies revealed dreadful internal injuries which resembled explosions. It caused sudden death, madness and even led to suicide and murder. It affected the youngest and healthiest in society and not, as might have been expected, the very young and very old as would have been the case in previous pandemics. Even stranger to relate was the fact that more women died in countries which had been involved in the war and more men in countries which had remained neutral throughout the conflict. And, never to forget, people were dying of this flu in every single part and corner of the entire world. There were those who firmly believed that the Great Flu was a payback for the huge sacrifice of the Great War itself. Some believed that it was nothing short of divine retribution.

Where did the flu first break out?

No one knows for sure but it could have been almost anywhere in the world. It could have something to do with the large movements of men in the European theatres of war. The truth still eludes the historians but many facts are clear. There were three distinct waves of the outbreak – summer and autumn of 1918 and the spring of 1919. The most severe, ironically, was at the time of the cessation of hostilities when the world was celebrating the end of the war. In Belfast, for example, the first wave coincided with the return of the surviving soldiers from Europe as they travelled together on the railways and cross channel ferries. Close proximity with other people seemed to be the catalyst in catching the flu. It also spread when these young men, having been bereft of entertainment throughout their days in the trenches, were at last enjoying themselves again at dances and football matches. Soon, sadly, all these venues and attractions were avoided – like the plague, of course. As more and more of these valiant and brave young men came home, fully expecting a rapturous reception, all they witnessed were empty streets and very unwelcoming surroundings. They were suspected of bringing the flu home with them from the stinking holes in the ground in the battlefields of Flanders, which had been their homes for so long.

The demography of the outbreak

By the end of the Great War in 1918 the flu was at its peak all over the world. Thousands were dying every day and, in Ireland, great pressure was being put on doctors, nurses, families and all the caring services. The death rate in Ireland was actually slightly higher than the average. In the last flu epidemic in 1892 those who died were either old or young but this time it was the young male population which suffered. It was also the case, strange as it may seem and sad too, that it wasn't the weak and vulnerable who succumbed but family breadwinners, young brides and the soldiers returning from war. Pregnant women died in large numbers and in Paris, as an example, 50% of them died in that dreadful year. Death rates in the workhouses, in mental hospitals and in schools were very high and visitors were not even allowed inside to see their dying relatives, again because of the risk of infection. In the various workplaces throughout every country, it was those workers who managed to avoid being stricken down who were then expected to do the extra work required owing to the absence, or death, of their colleagues. Clergy and those members of the professions who helped out above and beyond the call of duty were struck down too in great numbers and it didn't really matter whether you were rich or poor, if you caught the flu your chances of survival were remote. The farmers, who were expected to continue to provide foodstuffs for the shops, were not spared either. Those who escaped the infection had to milk their cows and bring in the harvest if they were still able to do so. If not, the people starved alongside those who were dying from the flu.

Strange to say, the medical profession seemed unable to discover a remedy; even stranger, it was said that the war had finished abruptly because the German soldiers were too ill to fire any more shells and, perhaps strangest of all, is that this time the poor were not blamed for spreading the disease as had been the case with the Great Famine.

How did towns and villages react to the pestilence?
The Great Flu shut down the ordinary workings of life. In Ireland, as elsewhere, businesses and shops closed, mail went undelivered,

doctors' surgeries shut down and dances and sports games were cancelled. There weren't enough people to organise funerals and those nurses who were still fit enough were overworked in their crowded hospital wards. Schools closed down, probably to the delight of the children, and church attendance was badly affected. Clergy from every denomination were totally overworked tending to the needs of their congregations. Courts were suspended and there was a marked increase in the consumption of alcohol, although many felt that this was one way of averting the flu. In fact as the time went on, many frightened folk took to drink and to carrying a piece of garlic in their pockets. Whether or not these remedies worked is another matter, but many did believe that they helped them avoid a premature death. Wakes for the dead, a strong tradition in Ireland, proved to be a problem for no longer were neighbours and even relatives attending as they feared that, by mixing closely in a tightly packed room around a coffin, they might become affected. Thus were communities throughout the land deprived of what was one of their most comforting traditions. Doctors, nurses and even the police had to bury the dead in many instances owing to the dearth of funeral directors who were a particularly vulnerable section in every community. And the worst horror of all was to return to your house, after just an hour or two, to find one of your close relatives, your son or your mother, lying dead on the floor.

Fear stalked the land

Although we are concentrating on the effects of the flu in Ireland, we must never forget that the instances described were replicated in every country in the world. People now started to shun others; normal social intercourse abruptly ceased; alarm and panic set in and localities throughout the country became ghost towns. In 1832, during an outbreak of cholera, those suffering, and their families, were ostracised as if, in some way, they had been responsible for bringing the disease to their home town. Although this did not happen during the flu epidemic, many locals tended to avoid their neighbours' houses where there were members suffering from the flu. So people didn't go anywhere lest they met an unfortunate who had the contagion or who had relatives who were afflicted. Those still unaffected avoided trams and trains; they kept out of shops and popular venues like pubs and cinemas and even kept away from church. When a death occurred, burials were carried out as swiftly as possible with friends of the deceased only making a very brief appearance at the graveyard. And the young soldiers returning from the war were avoided and many were even blamed for bringing the flu back from the trenches. Life in Irish localities became a wholly different scenario. People avoided and ignored their friends; the same people, who would always have come to the aid of a friend or neighbour, now made sure to pass them on the other side of the street if they were thought to have had the disease; life had changed and had changed irrevocably.

And there was no cure, or a medical one at any rate. The flu virus was only eventually isolated and named in 1933, fourteen years after the outbreak. Yet the authorities had the nerve to tell these frightened and panicked people to keep calm and not to panic. The fact that the medical profession took so long to pinpoint the cause was unsettling as this was the so-called 'golden age' of medicine when cures had recently been found to the likes of anthrax, rabies, diphtheria and tetanus. Doctors were astounded and confused at the state of the internal body organs and the speed of death. They were under terrific strain and, for a lonely place like the Aran islands where there was only ever the one doctor, life was intolerable as they tried to care for so many sick people on their own. Many doctors themselves died of the flu and they had little or no respite from their constant efforts to save as many people as they could. Nurses too were hard pressed although they did have valuable help from students and nuns and yet, despite their constant hard work, they did take time to consider how best to care for sick patients in future outbreaks. This surely was a truly commendable trait in their commitment to those suffering in their communities.

But how did the authorities react?
Most of the officials of the local authorities remained detached, ineffective, disinterested and disorganised. Those concerned with public health simply concentrated on containment of the outbreak and not the immediate relief that the population urgently needed. They were, as a result, lambasted for their insufficient action, but they asked what more could have been done. Some areas were well catered for whilst others were practically ignored. The provision of relief was just a lottery and many people felt abandoned. Had it not been for the doctors, nurses and the sterling work carried out by a number of women's voluntary organisations, many would simply have died without aid or succour. Private hospitals, the St Vincent de

Paul members and other charities also proved to be lifesavers for so many. Once the war was over and the flu epidemic had subsided by the late spring of 1919, a number of improvements in the workings of local authorities were introduced, although implementation in Ireland was delayed by the War of Independence and the Civil War which followed it.

Naming the disease and trying to prevent a recurrence

This was more than just a 'flu'. There had been such epidemics in the past but none had anything like the intensity of the present outbreak. It was given different names in different countries. Probably the first name was 'the Spanish Flu' and in Ireland it was 'the mysterious malady', 'terrible malady' or 'something like the flu'. But none of these descriptions in any way equated to its terrible and distressing effects on so many people all over the world. It was a misnomer if ever there was one. How could anyone just call it 'flu' when women and children just fell down and died; what name could you give to a killer disease which made young fit and healthy men go mad; what medical description could be given to an affliction such as this that made your skin turn black and you started bleeding from your mouth at a moment's notice. There is little doubt that its cause seemed to be in some way associated with the Great War and its filthy trenches and piles of unburied bodies spread all over the fields of Europe. But then fingers were pointed at possible reasons nearer home. Perhaps unclean streets, unhygienic tram cars and dirty train carriages could have been the source of the infections and, of course, there were those who firmly believed that it was God's judgment on man's immorality and wickedness in starting a war in the first place.

The horror of the flu ended as quickly as it had begun. By the early summer of 1919 life actually started to get back to normal – in America, Africa, Europe, and in Ireland itself. Changes were soon initiated to prevent any recurrence. People bought disinfectants to ward off what they called 'microbes' and personal cleanliness was emphasised. Pills and medicines were sold in vast quantities. This opened the door for many unscrupulous firms to overcharge for these vital potions and more and more life insurance policies were sold by companies out to make quick profits. Trains and trams and all public conveyances were enthusiastically cleaned and sanitised to prevent further infection. It was even the case that lots more bicycles were sold as it seemed better to ride your bike to your school or place of work rather than travel on a contaminated train.

Who will remember the Great Flu?

There were still people alive in Ireland in 1918 who remembered the Great Famine and, although many more died over that five year period, none of them would dispute the utter intensity of this outbreak. The question being asked by so many was 'if it was God's will, then would He ever send such a pestilence again?

There is a strange fact about this flu pandemic. People deliberately and quickly stopped talking about it; people were haunted by the memory of a disease that had killed so many of their loved ones; people all over the world, as in Ireland, had etched in their minds the blood, the bodies and the unattended wakes, but remained silent. As a consequence no stories have been passed down the generations making the Great Flu an almost completely unknown and totally forgotten tragedy. What is, of course, recalled is the horror of the Flanders fields and the dead of the Great War.

It is only in recent years that historians have started to write about this catastrophic event in Ireland's past. They inform their readers and encourage them to search hospital archives which do contain lots of information but which have remained unread since the days of the flu. The Great Flu had just fallen off the map of Ireland's history. Perhaps now, at last, is the time for this and succeeding generations to know and understand what horrors happened to members of their own families at that time.

Historians also remind us of the consequences which Ireland had to endure in the aftermath of the outbreak. Young men were still returning, often with significant injuries and suffering from post war traumas, by the time the flu had subsided. At home politicians of all shades and opinions were doing their best for their constituents and nor should it be forgotten that the War of Independence was raging. Whilst these men fought, many of the combatants were dying from the flu. Army, police and Republican personnel were affected. The point to remember is that, although we all know of what was going on in Ireland by way of the political struggles, we never knew that so many of the men and women involved were succumbing to the flu.

The conclusions

This horrific pestilence lasted but nine months and when it eventually subsided life carried on. People mourned their dead; they gave thanks for the exceptional work performed by the caring professionals and by the hard-working charities; they prayed that such a disaster would never visit the earth ever again. This 'tale of disaster', 'this tale of catastrophe' lodged in the minds of those who had suffered but they kept their thoughts to themselves. Whether you were rich or poor, lowly subject or gentry, the flu had hit every class and creed very hard. Lessons had to be learnt and, in most cases, improvements were made. Citizens all over the world had grieved and agonised. They remembered, but silently, those who had perished and quietly asked the question – could not something have been done to avert such a cataclysmic plague, epidemic and pestilence which they had endured for those nine dreadful months in 1918 and 1919?

Curious for more?

I can recommend these books for further reading:

Foley, Caitriona, *The Last Irish Plague – the Great Flu Epidemic in Ireland*, Irish Academic Press, 2011.

Barry, John M., *The Great Influenza – the Story of the Deadliest Pandemic in History*, Penguin, 2009.

For books that aren't in common circulation I may be able to source them for you. Email me at clive.scoular@gmail.com or check out my website – *clivescoular.com*.

German Spies in Ireland

Gunther Schutz, one of the German spies

THE OUTBREAK OF World War Two had many repercussions for the island of Ireland. Many of the population considered that the relatively infant Irish Free State would side with the Allies since many families in Ireland had long associations with the British fighting forces and the probability of young Irishmen joining up on the British side was high. And so it was that many tens of thousands did join the Royal Navy, the Army and even the Royal Air Force. The stage therefore seemed set for men and women from all parts of the island to join together to fight the Axis powers.

But a certain Eamon de Valera had other ideas and as soon as the war was declared he brought a motion before the Dail effectively taking the Free State out of the conflict before it had even started. The country, he declared, would remain neutral and so the so-called Emergency was introduced. Ireland south of the border would take no part in the world war. Many people were surprised; many were enraged and even more were actually relieved. How would Ireland's neutrality affect the Allied cause? After all Northern Ireland would be an integral part of the war effort and how would the tentative relations between the two states on either side of the border pan out?

Winston Churchill, not yet Prime Minister of course in September 1939, had plenty to say and he fairly bellowed his condemnation at what he saw as a cowardly act. He demanded back the former Treaty ports of Berehaven, Cobh and Lough Swilly which had just the year before been handed back to the Irish government. In the newspapers he tried to put fear into the hearts of all Irish men and women that the enemy would now find it easy to attack the British mainland from the cover of Irish ports. However sense prevailed as the days and months passed on. If the British did take back these ports they would have had to station thousands of British forces all round the entire coastline of the Free State and thus be accused of misuse of much needed manpower in the fight against the Nazi regime – why tie up forces in Ireland when they would be needed on the battlefields of Europe and north Africa?

The Free State had made its decision and for the duration of the war, de Valera was able to keep his fragile state out of the direct firing line. However history will also tell that, although he was officially neutral, he did turn a blind eye when it came to bringing aid and giving assistance to the Allied cause. But the Free State was also vulnerable in other ways.

The IRA

From the beginning of 1939 the IRA had been carrying out a bombing campaign in Great Britain. There had been over one hundred outrages causing at least one death and a number of injuries as well as damaging the London Underground system. Close to the outbreak of war five innocent people were killed in Coventry and two of those responsible were executed after a Prevention of Violence Bill was brought before the House of Commons. The British government was determined to stamp out such terrorist activity and their resolute action prevented any further IRA atrocities throughout the duration of the war. How then did de Valera react to these executions and the firm stance being taken by Westminster? He took an equally determined line. Much to the chagrin of many of his people, he introduced into the Dail energetic measures to curtail the activities of the IRA on Irish Free State soil. His actions proved even tougher than those applying throughout the United Kingdom and, during the war years, a number of IRA men were executed in Irish jails for their nefarious activities. It was never going to be said that de Valera was soft on the IRA – and many discovered this to their cost. And so the stage was set – how then would the two parts of Ireland fare during the battles and conflict to come?

The presence of enemy spies was well known throughout Great Britain. It would seem obvious that the enemy would do its best to infiltrate British soil – and so they did. During the war years over one hundred German spies entered Britain with a mission to inform their masters in Germany the state of British defences. Many were quickly discovered and condemned to prison cells; others did succeed in their objective as effective spies; yet more did cause a certain amount of disruption around Britain particularly within airfields and ports. But did any of these spies come to Ireland? Let's see as we examine the effectiveness, or otherwise, of those who did come to spy on neutral Ireland.

The German presence in Ireland at the outbreak of the war was minimal. There was a German minister who acted as ambassador, Dr Eduard Hempel, and he remained at his post in Dublin throughout the entire duration of the war. He was a level-headed diplomat and well liked by the Irish administration. He realised, perhaps more than many others around him, that he needed to keep contact with de Valera and his staff but he also knew that he needed to keep his head down. And in these endeavours he largely succeeded. He had a small staff at the embassy consisting of three counsellors and a few secretaries as well as members of his own family. He was the ideal man for the tricky task of keeping Berlin acquainted with what was going on but never being drawn into any kind of internal conflict. He did not want to jeopardise Irish neutrality and forbade, as far as he was able, any propaganda being disseminated from his office.

As Germany aggressively attacked the Allies and particularly the British during the first year of the war, there were a number of Irish citizens who would have described themselves as pro-German. However the majority were most definitely pro-Allies although not necessarily pro-British. They could not imagine the scenario of a German overlord despite many assessing the British as a pretty aggressive tyrant. But the German High Command still wanted to know who might support them in Ireland when their victory in Europe eventually came. They needed information and they knew that their only real supporters would be the IRA which, though now silenced in Great Britain, was still active in the Free State. There had been an audacious raid on the Magazine Fort in Phoenix Park in Dublin just a couple of days before the first Christmas of the war when a large number of lorries was driven to the fort which their occupants surrounded before holding the soldiers captive and making off with over a million rounds of ammunition. The strange thing – or the crazy thing – is that they did not take a single weapon although many were available. This attack caused an outrage in the country which led to an unbelievably speedy response from de Valera and his government. A countrywide search was quickly made and within a week all the ammunition was recovered in various dumps throughout the length and breadth of Ireland. And within another week the Dail had passed an Emergency Powers Act. This was one of the toughest pieces of legislation ever enacted by any Dublin administration and was to lead to several members of the IRA being executed.

The Germans were of course following these events staged by their supposed allies in Ireland. They were not impressed. They wondered, or perhaps were astonished, that the IRA should take this kind of action against their own people presumably knowing full well that this would alienate the ordinary men and women of Ireland. So what would the Germans do now?

Sending spies to Ireland

They decided to take a gamble. They wanted accurate information from Ireland regarding the movements of their enemy knowing perfectly well that Northern Irish territory belonged to that enemy. They also realised that the IRA was fairly ineffective but the Abwehr, the German military information-gathering organisation, did need to know what was happening in Ireland. They could not afford to be caught out. What follows can only be described as a catalogue of errors, blunders, faux pas and downright idiocy on the part of a nation whose determination it was to change the face of Europe forever. It is now up to you to make your own judgment on the German spy debacle in Ireland.

Oscar Pfaus seemed a good choice as the first spy to be sent to Ireland. He had spent many years in the United States and was fluent in English. He had returned to live in Germany in 1938 and had immediately joined the Abwehr. He may have been surprised when given his first assignment – he was to go to Ireland to liaise with the IRA although he, like his lords and masters, knew that there were no existing contacts with them. His was going to be a very difficult task and the only name he had upon arrival in early 1939 was that of General Eoin O'Duffy whose career had taken a nosedive in recent times. He had been the leader of the Blueshirts in Ireland; he had fought in the Spanish Civil War; he had even been Chief of Police in Cosgrave's government. But by now he was a nobody although at least he might be of some use to Pfaus. Clutching at straws, therefore, Pfaus approached him. Rather than welcoming him, O'Duffy reacted with horror and disbelief. He did not want to help the German but, after some encouragement, he did agree to give Pfaus some assistance although not by giving him any names. Eventually Pfaus was taken to meet the then leader of the IRA, Sean Russell, when he persuaded Russell to send an agent to Germany. All this seems incredible in that the IRA had never even thought of sending a man there themselves. They quickly sent Jim O'Donovan who became known as the IRA's 'official agent' to the Abwehr and the regime in Germany. Oscar had done his job and returned to his homeland.

Now that these somewhat tentative arrangements had been made and some information was flowing between the IRA and the Abwehr, the Germans decided to send another agent.

Ernst Weber-Drohl, who was also known as 'Atlas the Strong', was to be landed on Irish soil in the company of a radio operator and a radio. Things were looking promising until the radio operator decided to opt out. So Ernst set out by plane on his own, clutching the radio he knew nothing about. As he was being parachuted into Ireland, he let the radio slip from his grasp and it fell into the sea. So much then for the arrival of an agent, a radio operator and a radio. Ernst, however, realising that his task was now all the more difficult, still managed to make contact with Jim O'Donovan who had recently come back from Germany. The information that he gave the IRA man included notes and instructions for the IRA in Germany and the German spies in Ireland. O'Donovan was then arrested although Ernst's messages were never intercepted. In time Ernst was himself captured, then interned and finally released. He remained in Ireland for some time but he was followed by the Irish police whose job it was to spy on the spy. Ernst's work as an agent was over and he returned to Germany never knowing whether or not his work as a spy had been of any use to the Abwehr.

Hermann Goertz was a well-to-do and gifted German who had actually spent time both in England and in Ireland. It was said that he liked the Irish. He must have liked England too for, when he was visiting during the 1930s, he busied himself taking photographs of English airfields. This was, of course, illegal and he was soon to feel the force of English law when he was arrested and sent to prison for four years. He was released just before the outbreak of war in 1939 and immediately returned to Germany. Any photographs he had taken had presumably been sent home and would have proved very useful for the Luftwaffe. The Abwehr decided to sent Goertz to Ireland, an assignment which he relished. But rather than trying to make friends with the IRA in the Free State, whose authorities were severely clamping down on terrorist activity and even allowing IRA men to die on hunger strike in Irish jails, he was ordered to go to Northern Ireland to try to kindle rebellion amongst the IRA there with a view to tying up the British in the Province. This would be a most dangerous mission but one which appealed to him. In the meantime, however, the High Command kept delaying Goertz's flight to Ireland. When a meeting had finally been arranged with Sean Russell to be updated on the situation in Ireland, Goertz discovered that, on the very night the meeting was to take place, his plane for Ireland was ready and he had to leave. It would be true to say therefore that he left on a wing and a prayer.

But at least he was on board his plane for Ireland which was scheduled to land him somewhere in county Tyrone. When the green light on board his plane flashed, Goertz grabbed his radio and jumped out. As he parachuted down, his radio slipped and was lost forever. On landing he discovered very quickly that he was absolutely lost. Any road signs he saw did not relate to any of the county Tyrone towns or villages whose names were etched on his mind. When he did find out where he was, it was certainly not anywhere in county Tyrone. He had been dropped down to earth near Trim in county Meath which is not anywhere near the northern county. What did he do then? What happened next utterly defies logic. Lost, alone and without hope of finding either help or succour, he decided to swim across the river Boyne. For some reason he decided not to use the bridges which crossed the river close to Trim itself. The maps he had been carrying, and the invisible ink he had secreted on his person, were jettisoned and discarded. What was he to do as he dragged himself out of the river, soaked to the skin and still without a single idea in his head?

He did have one address in Ireland which he had committed to his memory – which was just as well with everything belonging to him now completely destroyed. He had been told that, if absolutely stuck, he was to secretly contact Francis and Iseult Stuart who lived near Laragh in the Wicklow mountains. The Stuarts (Iseult was the daughter of the feisty Republican lady, Maud Gonne, whilst her husband, Francis, was a well known author and literary guru whose sympathies were decidedly pro-German) would come to his assistance. At least he hoped so as he had nowhere else to turn. We can only surmise and wonder how an ill-equipped German gentleman, although proficient in the English language, could make his way on foot the almost one hundred miles which separates Trim from Laragh. There must have been some tricky enquiries as to the way to the next town or village; there must have been some astonished glances directed at this dishevelled traveller and there must have been utter disbelief when the Stuarts' door was opened upon this personage who, after all, turned out to be the German High Command's latest agent in Ireland. But the Stuarts warmly welcomed him, got him a change of clothes and provided him with his first nourishing meal for dear knows how long.

Iseult Stuart then took Hermann Goertz into Dublin to fit him out in a new suit of clothes. She then set about getting Goertz in touch with the IRA's Chief of Staff, a man called Stephen Hayes. Whatever information Goertz had for the IRA – and one wonders what he had to share with them since he had landed in Laragh with nothing except his wet attire – he discussed with Hayes and another IRA luminary, Stephen Held. Over the next days there was quite an amount of activity during which Held was arrested at his home in Dublin and during which time Goertz had managed to evade capture himself. The Irish police seemed to know that a German spy was in the vicinity but they failed to take him into custody. Meanwhile Iseult Stuart was questioned and brought to court to explain how Goertz's new clothes had been found at her house. She was able to give satisfactory answers and was released. But Goertz could no longer stay with the Stuarts so he did what all good spies would do, he went on the run, choosing the Wicklow hills as his hiding place. Whilst he shivered and starved as he evaded arrest, he concluded that the IRA was 'rotten to the core'. This seems somewhat of an understatement especially in these trying circumstances.

Goertz tried to get messages to the Abwehr, usually without any success. Although he had been forbidden to contact Dr Hempel, the ambassador in Dublin, he felt he had no other choice. Hempel agreed to meet him and some contact was made with Germany. His main point was that the IRA was utterly useless – something which his masters would already have known – and Goertz confirmed that the IRA, apart from being worse than useless, was not even trying to raise any money to help their associates. His parting shot was that the Irish knew how to die for Ireland but not how to fight for it. For the next number of months Goertz continued to evade capture and was actually able to make contacts with some of the Irish TDs and other people of influence – and still he avoided the police. Those he met were anxious to know how a victorious Germany would treat

Ireland. By now he had a place to stay in Dalkey, south of Dublin, and it was at this house that he met his visitors. The government of de Valera did not, however, have anything to do with these clandestine discussions and even accused Goertz of having actual invasion plans for the Free State which was, of course, quite untrue. But this must have been an interesting time in and around Dublin. From such a feeble and feckless start, Herr Goertz was certainly causing some feathers to be ruffled. He knew too that there would be rumours that, if and when the Americans joined on the Allied side, an invasion by the Allies might become a possibility. Goertz miraculously remained a free man but he knew something would have to happen soon or he would be captured. He got a message through to Germany requesting a plane to take him home so that he could report on his activities in Ireland to his superiors. But he was too late and he was taken into custody at the end of November 1941 having been at liberty for over nineteen months – which does seem almost incredible considering his inauspicious arrival in Ireland. He was taken to Mountjoy prison and was eventually interned at Athlone along with nine other German agents. Goertz didn't think much of Athlone, which he felt was gloomier and less comfortable than Mountjoy.

When the war came to an end the question was – what would Goertz decide to do? Most expected him either to want to return or be deported back to Germany. He decided otherwise and applied to be allowed to stay in Ireland. By the autumn of 1946 he heard that he would be permitted to remain and went to live with the Farrell sisters in Dublin. He even married in 1947 but, in April of that year, all former German agents were rearrested and deported. Hermann

Goertz could not face this embarrassing humiliation and committed suicide at the end of May 1947. He was buried in Dublin and thus ended the life of Germany's longest serving, and probably only, creditable spy that Germany sent to Ireland during World War Two.

Walter Simon and Willy Preetz were the next spies to be sent to Ireland and given the fairly straightforward task of sending weather reports back home to Germany. This information would have helped the Luftwaffe with their flying missions over different parts of the British Isles. Walter was landed by U boat off the south west coast and having stepped on to dry land, asked the first person he saw where Dingle railway station was. The only problem was that this person happened to be a policeman who immediately arrested this suspicious visitor and had him sent to Dublin where he received a three-year sentence in Mountjoy. The same thing happened to Willy who again asked the wrong person and found himself in jail alongside Walter Simon. So much for the German espionage system in Ireland and so there were no weather reports sent back by these two amateur spies – Irish police ten marks, German spies, no marks.

Gunther Schutz now entered the fray, stage right so to speak. He set off by plane from Germany to be parachuted into county Kildare near Newbridge but, like so many others, the pilot seemed to get his bearings wrong and Gunther found himself in New Ross in county Wexford. Anyway he had landed to get on with the task set for him – and that was to travel to Northern Ireland, to Belfast to be precise, to find out what he could about the warships being built there. This also seemed a reasonably attainable job except that, like most of his predecessors as Hitler's top spies, he immediately encountered two policemen and was arrested – so much for the vital information he was to find. He was interned in Sligo jail and soon afterwards was transferred to Mountjoy where he made friends with the other spies incarcerated there. Looking back on all these debacles, one would have assumed that heads would have rolled back at the High Command's offices in Germany – but there is no confirmation that this was the case. Schutz had fire in his belly and was determined to get out of prison so he hatched an escape plan. He somehow, presumably through some sympathetic guards, managed to ascertain the names and addresses of members of the IRA outside the jail. He inveigled a Dutch prisoner, one Jan van Loon, to work out how they could get out of a toilet window which was a scary 20 feet up a wall. Schutz bravely descended the massive wall, although Loon did not, and got clean away. He soon found a safe house which happened to be the home of Cathal Brugha's widow, Cathal having been an important name in the Easter Rising and the Civil War, during which he lost his life. Arrangements were well in hand for Schutz to be returned to occupied France in a boat from somewhere on the southern Irish coast. But just as he was preparing to leave, his luck turned against him and he was arrested by the police who, as it happened, weren't even looking for him. He was taken to Mountjoy where he met Hermann Goertz who didn't even know that Schutz had been sent to Ireland. They didn't much like each other but they had to make the best of their imprisonment along with another eight or so German prisoners. They were moved to Athlone jail which Schutz thought was a better place than Mountjoy. Like all good prisoners of war, the German spies made an attempt to tunnel out of prison but without success. In the end they were released from jail after the end of the war. Their days of spying for the Third Reich were over, but were, in truth, over before they had begun. The myth of a ring of effective and successful spies was finally blown – the story is just one of unadulterated farce and a true embarrassment to their lords and masters in Germany.

But there was still a sting in the tail. Sean Russell, the man sent to Germany to act on behalf of the IRA, also came to a sorry end. Whether or not he had been of any use to the IRA is doubtful and a matter of conjecture. When he needed to return to Ireland to report on progress, the Germans arranged for a U boat to take him home. He sailed from Wilhelmshaven in the company of another Irishman called Frank Ryan who had fought in the Spanish Civil War and who had been sentenced to death for his trouble. But during the journey, Russell became ill and died on board. He was buried at sea in sight of his homeland. Ryan then decided that he would return to Germany and, ever since, a question as to what actually happened to Russell has haunted those interested in this erstwhile 'IRA man in Germany'.

This whole story is surely a remarkable one; a story of incompetence; a story of stupidity; a story that surely defies belief.

Curious for more?

I can recommend this book for further reading:

Stephan, Enno, *Spies in Ireland*, London, Macdonald & Co., 1963.

For books that aren't in common circulation I may be able to source them for you.
Email me at clive.scoular@gmail.com or check out my website – *clivescoular.com*.

The Belfast Blitz

Destruction of a north Belfast street

IN THE FIRST two decades before the partition of Ireland in the early 1920s, the six counties of Ulster, soon to become Northern Ireland, were prosperous and thriving. The main industries of shipbuilding, spinning and rope making were, in fact, the leaders in their fields. Belfast had a growing population which had already exceeded 400,000. Life was good despite the political struggles of the time and the possibility of the country being divided.

But as soon as partition had become a reality, the hungry 20s hit the new Northern Ireland hard in the same way as it affected every country throughout Europe. The depression and rising unemployment became ugly features of life in the Province. The shipyards were not able to attract new orders and between the end of 1931 and the middle of 1934, not a single ship was launched at the normally busy yards. Workman Clark's 'wee yard' was forced to close leaving many men redundant. Fortunately for the Harland and Wolff yard, fortunes at last changed and orders started coming in again. There was a serious decline in the linen industry as well, not just because of a lack of orders, but because less material was needed to be manufactured on account of ladies wearing shorter skirts with the result that voluminous underwear was no longer required.

But all was not doom and gloom. The 1930s proved a turning point and by 1937 new industries were opening up, the best-known being the arrival of Short Brothers and Harland and their aircraft building enterprise. There was consequently more employment and life at home began to improve. Half the population now possessed a wireless set and one in seven families owned a car; one in four of the population weekly attended their local picture house and the men attended football matches and the greyhound racing at Celtic Park. There still were, however, many impoverished families living in poor housing which many thought was the fault of a seemingly corrupt and disinterested Belfast Corporation. The situation got so bad that, during the war, the Corporation was actually suspended and administrators brought in. There were still problems with the health and social care services for the needy amongst the population; TB was rife and there were too many curable diseases adversely affecting too many of the people. More needed to be done. All in all life in Northern Ireland, whilst beginning to improve, still had quite a way to go.

Preparation for war – was the Province ready?

Whilst war preparations were frantically being made in large towns and cities in Great Britain, there was an obvious and distinct lack of momentum and effort in and around Belfast and Londonderry. Belfast was, without doubt, the least protected city in the United Kingdom despite its shipyards and aircraft factories. There was a kind of lethargy within the government and a belief that a city this far north from Germany could not possibly be attacked in an air raid. There was probably an element of logic in this since Germany was so many miles away from Northern Ireland that their aircraft could surely never be able to carry bombs to such a far destination, drop them and then have sufficient fuel to return to their homeland.

But the government at Westminster did warn James Craig, the Northern Ireland Prime Minister, that Belfast should nevertheless be better prepared. This advice, however, largely fell on deaf ears. The city only had twenty anti-aircraft guns and had no fighter squadrons or even any barrage balloons. The construction of air raid shelters was practically non-existent with only four actually built and ready for use in the event of a raid. One of the problems about building shelters was the fact that the ground beneath the streets of Belfast was so close to the water table that it was well nigh impossible to dig into the ground far enough to construct anything, far less a shelter to protect the lives of the citizens of the city. The Northern Ireland government did pass air raid legislation but most people just ignored it. Too late then came the news, in the middle of 1940, that Germany had invaded France and the Low Countries, thus making a flight to Ulster so very much easier and shorter. In desperation, some trenches were frantically dug and the blackout enforced. All the citizens could do now was watch and pray.

The first air raid – 7 and 8 April 1941
During the early months of 1941 the Luftwaffe continued to bomb and devastate cities in England and Scotland. But, to date, there never had been a bomb dropped in anger on Northern Ireland. This was to change on the night of 7 and 8 April. That night hundreds of enemy aircraft were attacking various vulnerable locations in Great Britain. Some of them were bombing the shipyards on the Clyde and, perhaps with a few bombs still left in their bays, eight planes decided to head for Belfast thus finding themselves over Northern

Irish territory for the first time. The planes flew in low over the city and their targets were clearly the shipyards, which were easy to find owing to the absence of any onshore defences. The docks were hit as well as many of the local timber yards and commercial properties close to the city centre. Worst of all, a number of incendiary bombs fell on public housing both in the east and the north of the city. And, as the planes were departing having emptied their destructive load, they dropped a single bomb on one of Short's plane sheds, completely destroying 50 Stirling bombers which were almost ready for delivery to the Royal Air Force.

A total of thirteen people had been killed in the raid as well as all the destruction of many crucial targets throughout Belfast. The people of the city were bewildered and their complacency utterly dispelled. The enemy war machine had discovered their home town. Would the bombers return in greater and deadlier numbers? At Stormont the next day, it was hinted that the Prime Minister and his Cabinet were having a meeting and that no mention of the previous night's attack was even made. If this was true it does clearly epitomise the lack of concern and preparation to protect the citizens of this vitally important city.

The Easter Tuesday raid – 15 and 16 April 1941

When the German planes, which had struck Belfast with such force, returned to their bases in occupied France, their commanders would certainly have discussed the possibility of a specific raid on this eminently defenceless, yet important, target with all its heavy industries which were so vital to the war effort. And so it transpired that, just over a week after the first attack, Belfast, unprepared as it surely was, became the sole target for nearly 200 aircraft. Many stories are still related to this day of the swarm of droning German planes coming over the coast of county Down and approaching the city from over the Castlereagh hills.

On arrival over the docks hundreds of magnesium flares were dropped on parachutes which lit up the entire city. There was considerable damage caused to the shipyard and the aircraft factories, which resulted in a marked decrease in production of both ships and planes for the war effort. The main telephone exchange was hit and there were so many fires and conflagrations that the fire service could not cope with the destruction, very often not having a sufficient water supply or even enough lengths of hose. In the early hours of the morning of the 16th with the raid in full spate, John MacDermott, the Minister of Public Security, after discussion with his cabinet colleagues, decided to contact the Free State government to ask them for assistance from their fire service. Quickly Eamon de Valera, some say after some prodding from Cardinal McCrory in Armagh, gave the order to send 70 men and thirteen fire appliances north. Again there are memories from people alive today who recall the screaming fire engines speeding up the county Down roads to Belfast. When they arrived, they had an immediate problem. Their hose attachments did not fit the local Belfast hydrants and so it took some further precious time to find the necessary adaptors to allow them to get on with their job of extinguishing the fires. These men, along with the local firemen, carried out their difficult and dangerous task with expertise and bravery and their actions saved many lives.

But the true horror of that night was the fact that so many thousands of private houses were flattened and hundreds of innocent civilians killed. Entire streets were demolished and, in one dreadful incident, the York Street mill, many stories high, received a direct hit and collapsed on top of two streets beneath, completely obliterating them and causing dozens of deaths. During that night many of the older parts of the city were destroyed. Wilton's Funeral Home in the north of the city was also hit and dozens of their horses killed. Hospitals were overwhelmed with casualties and even the Ulster Hospital in Templemore Avenue was hit and badly damaged although their nursing and medical staff worked valiantly in the midst of this carnage dealing with so many deaths and injuries.

The aftermath

Those who survived this night of untold horror and mayhem could only stand and stare when day dawned. The Prime Minister himself, John Andrews, could only do the same. He travelled around the city witnessing the destruction first-hand and commiserating with the survivors. There wasn't a lot anyone could do. There was little electricity or gas and the shops, which were still standing, had little food left on their shelves. Every statistic was shocking. 500 houses had been destroyed or damaged beyond repair; 20,000 people were homeless; 500 streets had either been completely obliterated or were unrecognisable. Families searched the debris in the hope of finding their missing relatives or their bodies. The authorities opened up temporary morgues. Very quickly the spaces in the city's main mortuaries were filled and so a number of the city's swimming baths were pressed into service. Again this was a very surreal sight – bodies, in many cases badly disfigured, spread out in the pool area where many of the locals had been enjoying their weekly swim the day before. When as many of these bodies as possible had been identified, they were released to their families for burial. Those corpses that remained were taken to St George's market and laid out in the hope that their grieving relatives would be able to identify them. For days thereafter the city streets, churches and cemeteries were constantly filled with sorrowing friends and relatives following countless funeral processions as they said farewell to their loved ones cut down in the prime of their lives by an unseen, remorseless and callous enemy. Sadly many bodies were not identified and their remains were buried in common graves in the various city cemeteries.

Although the exact number of those killed that April night remains uncertain, most consider that 950 of Belfast's citizens were killed and many hundreds more injured. This represented the highest number of people killed in any one German raid throughout the war on any British city, apart from London itself. This truly is a startling statistic and a sobering one.

The locals head for the hills

Within a couple of days of the air raid, another extraordinary scene was witnessed in all parts of the city. People were starting to gather up their belongings and piling them onto a bicycle or cart or into a car if they owned one. They headed for the hills – chiefly to the side of Cave Hill and the slopes nearby. They began to sleep under hedges or in a farmer's shed if they were lucky. In the morning they returned to their homes and then repeated the procedure every evening afterwards for months to come. They became known as the 'ditchers'. The government officials saw what was happening, understood why it was happening, yet took ages to do anything to help them. Eventually they did arrange for some Nissen huts to be constructed to improve the somewhat squalid sleeping arrangements for those too frightened to return home permanently. After some months most of the 'ditchers' did return to their own homes but the fear of another attack remained.

There were many other people from the city who deserted their homes permanently and went to live in other parts of the country. As many as 100,000 people left Belfast at that time, leaving many localities almost bereft of any householders. Many of these evacuees foisted themselves upon folk in country towns and villages rather to the bemusement and displeasure of their reluctant hosts.

The fire raid - 4 and 5 May 1941

But the bombing was not over. On the night of 4 May a huge number of German planes, perhaps as many as 200, flew in over Belfast. This time they dropped 6,000 bombs and countless incendiaries on and around the aircraft factories; this time they sank three newly completed corvettes at their moorings in Harland and Wolff's yard; this time they wrecked more residential property and this time they killed another 190 people. The population was terrified yet again and felt despondent and depressed. They were beginning to fear that these three raids might just be the start of a continuous campaign of attrition to wipe Belfast off the map.

Once again the next morning the citizens examined with dismay the destruction wreaked upon their city. Many more homes had been destroyed and even their City Hall's banqueting hall and other parts of the city centre had been badly damaged. Disruption to the water supply during the raid meant that buildings, which could otherwise have been saved, had been burned to the ground. But once again the Dublin fire crews raced north to assist in extinguishing the fires. They had carried out a valiant service which the people of Belfast greatly appreciated. The newspapers carried many stories of the city's vain attempts to ward off the enemy. They also noted, probably with a rueful grin, that Parliament Buildings at Stormont, which had been covered in dark coloured tar to prevent its being a sitting duck in such an attack, had not only survived but had not even been attacked. Furthermore the famous statue of Edward Carson, close to the front of Stormont, which had also been protected previously, was undamaged. There were presumably debates, maybe heated debates, about the efficacy of spending money to care for these locations instead, perhaps, of putting more money into shelters and other protection for the population of Belfast.

However by the time of this third raid, many of the population, as we have already noted, had chosen to leave the city and find accommodation either in the hills above Belfast or far away in the countryside. The 'ditchers' remained, during the night, in their sheds or barns for many more months and it was the late autumn before most of them returned to their homes – that is, if they had a house to which to return. The citizens of Belfast were saddened when they heard that the Germans had even bombed neutral Dublin at the end of May and, in the raid, 34 people had been killed including four relatives of one of the brave Dublin firemen who had come to Belfast's rescue barely a month beforehand.

By now the government at Stormont had at last improved the city's defences with more shelters and more available aircraft stationed at Aldergrove. They even opened a new airfield at Ballyhalbert on the Ards peninsula. You might say that they were finally ready to repel any future attacks. But there were no more raids on Belfast. For a time, of course, the population was expecting more attacks but it was at this very time, towards the middle of 1941, that Adolf Hitler decided to turn his attentions to the east and to Russia. It was this dramatic change of strategy that saved Belfast, as well as all the already suffering English and Scottish cities, from yet more destruction.

The toll of lives and the state of the economy in the later war years

In the three raids on Belfast, over 1,100 people had lost their lives. Forty churches and a similar number of schools had been destroyed and as many as 23,000 new houses were needed to rehouse many thousands of Belfast's citizens. Industry had suffered badly but the shipyard and the aircraft factories were able to return to full production remarkably quickly. The statistics speak for themselves – 170 warships and 54 merchant ships built; 3,000 ships repaired or converted; over 500 tanks and 13 million aircraft parts built at Harland and Wolff; 1,200 Stirling bombers and 125 Sunderland Flying Boats constructed at the Short Brothers and Harland;